UNFOLLOW

QUESTION EVERYTHING
WITH EXCITEMENT

MELISSA M. WIGGINS
AKA COACH MUMMABEAR

LANDON
HAIL
PRESS

Paperback ISBN: 978-1-959955-24-5
Hardback ISBN: 978-1-959955-25-2
Cover design by Rich Johnson, Spectacle Photo
Published by Landon Hail Press

Dedicated to my Gran Jeannie in heaven,
the most joyful example of how to
really live your ONE.Life, in spite of circumstances.
Thank you for being the inspiration behind
what it really means to UnFollow. I love you.

TABLE OF CONTENTS

FOREWORD 1

INTRODUCTION 5

CHAPTER 1: UnFollow Medical Gaslighting 9

    THE WORK: Follow Question Everything With
    Excitement 22

CHAPTER 2: UnFollow Self-Imposed Prisons 24

    THE WORK: Follow Freedom 34

CHAPTER 3: UnFollow Blame 36

    THE WORK: Follow I am Responsible 42

CHAPTER 4: UnFollow Lassies who Lunch 44

    THE WORK: Follow Women Who Walk Win 49

CHAPTER 5: UnFollow Autopilot 53

    THE WORK: Follow Airplane Mode 59

CHAPTER 6: UnFollow Bullying our Bodies 61

    THE WORK: Follow Learning to Love our Bodies 69

CHAPTER 7: UnFollow Diet Culture 71

    THE WORK: Follow Intuitive Eating 75

CHAPTER 8: UnFollow Fix all the Trauma 77

    THE WORK: Follow Break Generational Trauma, One
    Trauma at a Time 82

CHAPTER 9: UnFollow Martyrdom Mountain 84

    THE WORK: Follow the Path to an EMPOWERED.Life ... 91

CHAPTER 10: UnFollow Parent Pleasing 92

THE WORK: Follow Your Inner Knowing 100

CHAPTER 11: UnFollow Boundary Blowups 101

THE WORK: Follow Boundary Blessings 108

CHAPTER 12: UnFollow Failure 110

THE WORK: Follow Winning or Learning 118

CHAPTER 13: UnFollow Perfectionism 119

Perfectionism 132

THE WORK: Follow Start Before You Are Ready 137

CHAPTER 14: UnFollow Raising Spoiled, Entitled Brats 138

THE WORK: Follow Family 144

CHAPTER 15: UnFollow Divorce 146

THE WORK: Follow Rebuild 159

CHAPTER 16: UnFollow Work-Life Balance 162

THE WORK: Follow Work-Life Alignment 171

CHAPTER 17: UnFollow Blowing out *Her* Candle 172

Thought-Detox and SPEAR 174

THE WORK: Follow Brain Training 177

CHAPTER 18: UnFollow Words 181

Sunshine Lollipop 185

THE WORK: Follow The Energy 188

CHAPTER 19: UnFollow Decision Fatigue 190

Asking for Help and Saying *No* 194

Sleep 195

THE WORK: Follow Outsourcing Decisions 200

CHAPTER 20: UnFollow Everyone 202

THE WORK: Follow You 210

ACKNOWLEDGMENTS..212

KEYNOTE SPEAKING & COACHING............................216

Retreats...216

Coaching and a Cup of Tea with Mummabear.................216

Social Media...217

Show Us Your Action..217

Don't Just Read. Act..218

TESTIMONIALS...219

Keynote Speaker Testimonials..................................219

Coaching Testimonials...221

ABOUT THE AUTHOR...225

FOREWORD

You're struggling.

And in the solitude of your quiet spaces. You know this. There is no hiding, when you are alone. So, while you may have subscribed to or followed beliefs, norms, and ideals for decades, there is a part of you that desperately wants to UnFollow the unwritten rules and ways of being that you've subjected yourself to. They've become a misery-making, self-imposed prison that eventually can't be covered up by enough pretending, posing, social media filtering, and "I'm fines." Maybe you are accustomed to a life of people-pleasing, being a busybody, perfectionism, balance, hiding, or some other concept you've unconsciously followed for a long time. Today, this deserves not only to be questioned, but questioned with excitement, as Melissa shares.

When you wholeheartedly dive into reading the pages of *UnFollow*, just know this: you won't be able to follow the same path in the same way, ever again. You will see what's been unseen, and once it's in view, there is no delete button, no rewind, no unsee-it mode, and you will be changed. Oddly enough, you know this is what you want. What you need. We all desire both safety and the known, *and* also, the unknown and adventure. Questioning everything with excitement gives you a fresh perspective on everything you've bought into, without even realizing it, and the tools to change it.

I remember exactly where I was the evening that I met Melissa. We were sitting around a large dinner table at a gorgeous restaurant, with a table full of the most beautiful and brilliant women, and we locked eyes as we sat directly across from each other. With her colorful outfit and wide-brimmed hat, this Scottish lassie made an impression, to say the least.

We were both scheduled to speak at the event, and the next day, as she spoke, I knew. I knew we were the same. We were A Mum And... A concept she not only teaches but models. A woman who won't use her children or the cards life has dealt her to hold her back. A woman who chooses to be a model, not a martyr. A woman I could relate to.

The uniqueness of her story, though, lies in her utter joy in sharing the messy middle, the twists and turns that are so real for us all, without the weight of shame. Her brave "I did that" way of sharing stories gives freedom to you, the reader, the same way it did to me, that first day I heard her speak on stage.

Freedom, after all, is what we desire on the deepest levels. And I should know. A mum of six kids, myself, I built a seven-figure business in just over two years, added in a second then a third six-figure business, and all in a span of four years, while raising babies, nursing babies, and having babies. It was like performance and perfectionism on steroids when I was in my late thirties and early forties, mixed with a whole lot of feeling incapable, inadequate, and afraid. Having now done THE WORK to grow and heal, just like you are about to do in this book, I've learned that success doesn't have to come at a price too high to pay. As an established coach, speaker, community builder, and leader, I can say this without a doubt:

You must UnFollow what is killing you.

Melissa's poignant stories, client examples, and tangible, applicable tools are essential for unwinding the narrative you've told yourself for far too long. Whether you've taken your last stand on Martyrdom Mountain, are so sick and tired of feeling like a failure, or if you're finally ready to tackle that big dream, she will guide you through to the truest version of you.

And her greatest gift she offers? An example of living full out, bearing her heart wide open, and telling you truths, about her and about you, that you need to hear. I've watched her with her kids, I've watched her take the stage, I've watched her champion other speakers from the audience. As someone who has been championed by her, I can confidently say, *UnFollow* is her way of championing all of you.

Whether you read this book as a family, a couple, a team, or gift this book to your teenager, *UnFollow* is for you. This lassie is a gift, too. She's ambitious, healing, and a whole-hearted human. Get ready to laugh, cry, and go on a wild ride through the pages of this book, which is guaranteed to leave you better than it found you.

If there's anything we all need now more than ever, it's the real, the raw, and the true EMPOWERED.Life that Melissa offers us in *UnFollow*. Along with the exciting concepts she teaches inside this book, including, ONE.Life, what are you going to do with it?

Melissa, I love how big you love! I love how big you live! You are creating ripples today and always.

Love,

Brooke Hemingway
Speaker, Coach, and Community Builder

*"Some people die at 25
and aren't buried until 75."*

—Benjamin Franklin

?

INTRODUCTION

Hellllooooooo, Lassies and Lads!
Welcome, brave souls, to *UnFollow: Question Everything with Excitement*, a book that promises a journey of transformation. I'm your guide: a Scottish motivational speaker, lawyer, life coach—A Mum And.

In the age of social media, the word *UnFollow* resonates with most of us as a simple digital action. It symbolizes detachment from someone's online life, a choice to mute their narrative from our daily scroll. If only real life was this easy. But what if it could be?

Imagine your life as a social feed, cluttered with belief systems, societal expectations, family norms, and self-imposed limitations. What if you had the power to curate this feed? To curate your real life, not just your Instagram feed. To *UnFollow* what doesn't serve you and make space for what truly matters?

> You are healing—but are you living?

You have ONE.Life—what are you going to do with it?

Through the chapters ahead, you'll discover how to reclaim your narrative, enabling you to live—truly live—in a generation of people who have become experts in healing but forgotten to live with energy and joy, and in spite of circumstances. You are healing—but are you living?

‽

Whether you're painfully grappling with the constructs of divorce, chasing the elusive shadow of perfectionism, wrestling with establishing healthy boundaries, pursuing meaningful goals, or anything in between, consider this book your survival kit for the soul. It's packed with practical tools and introspective exercises designed to help you *UnFollow* what doesn't serve you and *Follow* your own path.

Make no mistake: this book is more than a collection of words. It tackles the very areas of life that often tip us off the metaphorical beam, because this life is about living, not simply surviving.

The essence of this book is about asking the right questions. We often ask questions from a place of shame or guilt, but what if we've been doing it all wrong? What if we start asking questions from a place of excitement for a future—one we get to define? A future where we choose our favorite version of our life, not the one we have been living to date.

Each chapter is not a directive but a doorway to THE WORK—the deliberate choices about what to follow and *UnFollow*. It won't be easy, but this book is written to hold your hand, and it's got you until you've got you.

I've navigated my way through addictions, survived my child's stage 4 cancer diagnosis, and expanded my family through adoption. I can tell you firsthand that joy and energy are choices we make, regardless of the circumstances that try to define us. Intertwined with my own life journey, you'll find the stories of ten of the bravest people I know: my clients, who have also embarked on this transformative path, each contributing their unique experiences with the sole purpose of helping you, the reader and doer. Each client has been doing THE WORK, questioning with excitement, and using the tools I designed, which are laid out in this book.

This book is for everyone—it's for the teenagers grappling with identity in a digital world, for the lassies and lads balancing the demands of adulthood, for families seeking unity in a fragmented society, and for companies aiming to build a culture that thrives on individuality and collective purpose. Whether you're sixteen or sixty, a stay-at-home parent or a CEO, *UnFollow: Question Everything with Excitement* offers invaluable insights and tools that can transform the way you interact with the world, making it a must-read for anyone eager to take the reins of their own life, their family's or their company's.

Disclaimer: THE WORK has consequences. The people in this book who have done THE WORK have had a myriad of results. One has moved thousands of miles from the only place they knew, and one moved from the city to the beach and started an adventure company. Another client took their first real vacation in their career, and others have renegotiated the family chores in a two-parent working home. One couple came back from the cusp of divorce and are happier than ever. One thing is for sure: read this book, do THE WORK, and you will have the opportunity to never be the same.

P.S. This life WORK doesn't stop when the book closes. I invite you to join our brave and beautiful community online, to share your wins, your goals, and what you plan to *UnFollow*, with the hashtag #*unfollow*.

Let's make this interactive and collectively rewrite the narrative of what life should look like. Let's be a clan of leaders who live a value-driven and aligned life. It is time for our outside world to match our inside world. A clan of leaders who choose wisely in this ONE.Life.

This book is a toolkit for all who dare to scrutinize the status quo. I'll put the kettle on and make a cup of tea as we tackle the things that have taken us off the beam for far too long. It's time to *UnFollow*, lassies and lads.

Visit melissawiggins.life/unfollow to download your free UnFollow Workbook and start your journey of Questioning everything with Excitement!

Ready? Go Big or Go Home.

Love,
Coach Mummabear

CHAPTER 1

UnFollow Medical Gaslighting

"The man who asks a question is a fool for a minute, the man who does not ask is a fool for life."

—Confucius

OMG, OMG, OMG! It's positive, it's positive. I am going to be a mum.

I was twenty-six and elated. Is it weird that I still have that little pee stick? As a non-hoarder—as in, I throw away and donate everything I can on a weekly basis—it may speak to the depth of significance I felt, seeing that little stick turn pregnant. Those two little lines changed everything.

Like every other millennial, I couldn't wait to elaborately share the news with my husband. I did so by showing him the pee stick. Props to this generation behind me, videoing and dancing, scavenger hunting and creating elaborate ways to share the news with their people—truly, hats off. And also, thank you, God, for making me an eighties kid.

Laboring Cannon was quite the adventure.

Hi, nice to meet you. I am the first-time mum who knows zero about birth pain, but here is my completely natural birth plan. Imagine the nurse eyerolls that accompanied that request.

Physical pain is not my area of thriving. I am more of a mental pain-type of lassie. So, the fact that I thought I could give birth with no epidural was quite hilarious to my mum, sister, stepdaughter, and husband. But listen, in my defense, I

?

had been walking daily with an empty stroller and my dog—yes, it was as ridiculous as it sounds—listening to my deep-breathing birthing music, and darn it, I would do this thing naturally. My mum had birthed five out of her vagina, for God's sake, and not one drug. I could do this! Surely, it was in the genes?

I am here to confirm it was not in the genes.

On August 10, Cannon made his way into the world via C-section; after I tried to labor for five days and then was told, essentially, my vagina wasn't going to do her job, and this baby was not coming out of said vagina. Around 5:00 a.m., he was cut out of me.

P.S. Highly recommend a C-section. The whole attempting for days to give birth, being given Pitocin to bring on labor, and taking no epidural made me feel like I was dying. P.S.S. If you are reading this, have a birth plan, and you plan on doing no epidural, just know I'm rooting for you.

As someone who was formerly adamant that children were not in the cards for her, that my career as a lawyer was too important and all I wanted was to make partner, I was a pretty killer mum. This kid of mine was a chunky, happy, energetic bundle of chub. Raising kids in a country and city where you don't have any family and are new to challenges didn't stop me and that kid from living life like no tomorrow. His life was magical, and our time together changed me.

My career was still a major focus. I just started my own company, instead of working for someone, and this allowed me the time I deeply desired with Cannon. In every photo of that kid, he is smiling. And I imagined I could never love anyone more than this kid. So long as you fed him regular, and I mean a lot and often, he was happy.

When he was around a year and a half old, I noticed he had a little limp. As a first-time mum, I wasn't hyper-cautious with him, but I was super-aware of changes in his mood or movement. So, I did what most new mums do and took him to the pediatrician. Three visits later, the pediatrician said it was either growing pains or Cannon had bumped his leg when jumping in and out of the pool. He was a fierce little swimmer. "Boys will be boys," he said.

My husband was working away, and I was only two years into living in the U.S., and I realized medical practice is very different in the USA, compared to Scotland. The whole insurance card, providers, and a million different specialists really is hard to wrap your head around for the average European. But wrap my head around it I must. Cannon had reverted back to crawling due to the pain in his leg.

Watching this chubby, thirty-two-pound monster crawl around was comical but scary. I questioned the doctor, and while I was a new mum with no family in the country, I felt I needed another opinion. It is important to note here that while I was a new mum, I was also a lassie in her twenties who was programmed as a good girl, to respect authority figures, and a diehard people-pleaser. It was not easy for me to ask for specialist recommendations or to question a doctor. I left nauseated and scared the doctor wouldn't like me.

A few specialists later, Cannon was being pried from my arms for an X-ray. I couldn't go with him, as I was thirty-eight-weeks pregnant with our twin boys. With the twins on the way and moving from being a mum of one to a mum of three boys under the age of two, I had been spending all my time with Cannon, making our last solo months together count. Disney was our second home, and despite the fact that it felt like the twins might come out when I walked, it didn't matter. This was Cannon's and my time together. Memories must be made.

So, an X-ray, while my child was screaming and I couldn't be beside him, was not part of my Mumma and Cannon adventure plans.

I thought, "This is the worst day of my life." Hearing him scream was torture. They were attempting to keep still an active eighteen-month-old boy *and* take a picture... I guess boys will be boys.

The doctor showed me the scans and said, "This is osteomyelitis, an infection in his knee. We need to do surgery straight away, and he will be in a cast."

My inner dialogue went something like this:

"What the actual *****?! **** ****** *******"

A kid in a cast and twin newborns? My husband wasn't even in town. I called him to fly home immediately and get to the hospital in time for the surgery.

On Friday night, Cannon was sitting in a crib and had not eaten all day—this thirty-two-pound monster of mine had gone past the point of hangry and was in full-on rage mode.

My husband flew in and came straight to the hospital, where he and I draped over the crib on either side, attempting to soothe our son, but failing.

One of my superpowers is being intuitive: body language, tone, hand gestures—I can feel the energy. I carefully watched the doctor on the phone as he talked about Cannon, and a wave of fear took over my body. It felt like I had been electrocuted; something was wrong. We had been waiting to go to surgery, but something told me that wasn't happening.

I looked to Michael and said, "You don't think he has cancer in his leg, do you?"

I have no idea where in my brain those dreaded words came from. They were out before I could even reframe them.

Horrified, my husband looked at me said, "Why on Earth would you say that?"

I was equally horrified. I am the half-full girl, and he is the half empty—this isn't how we operate. We often joke that I am the optimist and he is the realist. Still, on that day, I don't know why I thought that or felt that, but I did.

The doctor walked toward me, as if in slow motion. I heard each step, one after the other. It felt like it took a lifetime for him to reach the crib where we stood.

The doctor had a friendly face and a soft demeanor. He gave us a wry smile and softly said, "We won't be doing the surgery. The blood work doesn't match up with what I would see if there was a true infection. I am going to keep him overnight and have some specialists visit through the night and tomorrow."

My stomach was in my throat, and I quieted the noise in my head that kept saying, *This is very bad.*

"What specialists?" I responded.

He listed off many, and somewhere in there said the word no one ever wants to hear as an adult, but especially not for your child: "*oncology.*"

I was familiar with the word oncology and the impacts of it. It had stolen my auntie at age thirty-two, leaving her three sons without a mother. We have all raised money for leukemia ever since. My Aunt Maxie was an angel on Earth and the ripple effect of her death is still felt today.

I still remember, at age ten, my cousin, Joseph, and I sitting on our uncle's/her husband's knees, and him telling us she had died. Joseph was the youngest son, and we were in school class together. It was heart-wrenching. I often say, "Kids need their mums, and mums need their kids." My Auntie Maxie and my son, Cannon, taught me that.

The token specialists came and went; they examined Cannon and wrote notes, scheduled tests, and left. Then, the oncologist came, somewhere in the middle, so as not to freak out a very pregnant mum and a dad. Either that or many of our besties worked at the hospital, and the fact that Cannon was there started to float around the various hospital floors. I wasn't on social media in 2013, but I was blessed to have some of the smartest friends who were key figures in the hospital we were in.

We were all exhausted. My husband and I lay on a pullout bed with our backs against the white-speckled hospital wall as our toddler slept in an unfamiliar bed for the first time. In the corner of the room, his little arm was bandaged up from the blood they had taken, and he was red-faced from exhaustion. My little chubby guy was spent.

The phone rang in the room, startling both Michael and me. On the other end was the shift nurse. The floor was quiet. It was late, really late now. It was dark. In the last several hours, Cannon had sat on my knee, cuddling my enormous belly, while we were wheelchaired from scan to scan, machine to machine. Each machine was more terrifying than the last.

"Hello?"

"Hi. It's nurse Kelly. The doctor is on the phone and wants to speak to you."

The doctor was the oncologist who had ordered a myriad of tests.

"Hi, Doctor."

"Hi. So, your son doesn't have osteomyelitis. I believe he has neuroblastoma."

I gasped. "What is neuroblastoma?"

I had never heard this word. I knew it wasn't good, but I was confused.

"It's an aggressive form of cancer."

....

The world stopped.

I couldn't breathe.

I felt like an elephant was on my chest.

I took the phone from my ear and slammed it into my husband's chest, saying, "You need to speak to him." And I ran out of the room.

I had a full-on panic attack and felt like I couldn't breathe.

I called my mentor, Miss Mary, and she talked me off the ledge. She went straight into fight mode and started making calls to find out what this meant.

That night, I lay awake on the pullout bed, just staring at my son's crib. His little hand hung out between the crib bars. He looked sad, even as he slept.

7:00 a.m. rolled around. I was sitting on the edge of the pullout bed with the room door wide open. Cannon lay asleep in the crib in the corner. Michael was sitting beside me, rubbing my back, after I'd had little to no sleep. My whole body ached, not just from being pregnant but the trauma of the last week that had led us there, sleeping in a strange room.

It was Saturday, April 19, 2013.

Walking slowly toward the room was a short man. He was gray-haired, perhaps around seventy years old. As he got closer to our room door, I recognized him. He was the man who pushed on Cannon's belly. He was the one who ordered the middle-of-the-night tests. He was the man who told me over the phone my son had cancer.

"May I come in?" he asked. His voice wasn't loud or quiet, not soft or friendly. His face wasn't kind. His energy felt very matter-of-fact.

He pulled up a chair and sat a few feet away from Michael's and my faces. "The tests confirmed it. Your son has stage-4 neuroblastoma cancer. His scans show his body lit up like a Christmas tree. The cancer is everywhere."

I word vomited these words that no mother ever wants to say: "Yeah, but he won't die, will he?"

In a very matter-of-fact way, he shrugged his shoulders, scrunched up his face, and said, "50/50."

His words pierced my heart, although I'm doubtful he knew that.

He continued on. "This is the most aggressive form of pediatric cancer, and it will be a long, hard battle for your son. He will need chemo, surgery, stem-cell transplant, immunotherapy, and radiation." That same doctor would later tell me that the chemotherapy Cannon needed would be "garden variety," meaning it was adult chemo for other forms of adult cancers.

During this season of my life, my people-pleasing began to die.

As a then twenty-something-year-old, I had always been taught to respect my elders. Yet, this seventy-year-old who was in charge of the entire department led me here:

TO QUESTION EVERYTHING!

?

Like all kids with neuroblastoma, the surgery, although only one part of the treatment, was extremely significant. Attempting to get a hundred percent of the cancer is not something many surgeons can do.

The gray-haired doctor told me I should use the hospital surgeon. Yet, when I question the surgeon, he said he cannot get all of the tumor from the abdomen area and has had only three or four cases like Cannon's. Yet this was who the gray-haired doctor suggested? My tendencies to accept what people say and not question everything had to be smashed. It was time to do my homework.

I did what law school taught me: I researched. I'd stay up all night, every night, reading parent blogs and trolling hospital websites. I came across a surgeon at Memorial Sloan Kettering Cancer Center. Dr. LaQuaglia. After mountains of paperwork, he requested that we fly to New York City to meet with him, and so we did. Cannon stayed at the local hospital, and my husband and I flew up for twenty-four hours and back.

"How many surgeries like Cannon's have you done?"

"Well, Cannon's is one of the most complex I have seen in my career. The tumor is wrapped around every organ and down into his hips. It's extensive, and I don't think I can get it out in one surgery. But on average, I do around eighty surgeries similar in nature each year."

I asked a question that got stuck in my throat at first, but I knew I needed to ask it. "Have you ever lost any children?"

"Yes. Three. Would you like to know their names and what happened?"

Tears rolled down my face.

This was our guy.

We returned to the hospital in Orlando and told the gray-haired seventy-year-old male doctor that we planned to do surgery in New York. He explained in a condescending manner that we were making a mistake. Over the course of our treatment, three and a half years, we would, in his mind, make many mistakes.

Eighteen months later, my son had treatment at Children's Hospital of Philadelphia, because our local hospital did not have a stem-cell transplant unit or proton-beam radiation therapy, both of which would significantly enhance our son's chances of survival. He had completed his surgery and countless doses of chemotherapy. He had been taken as close to death as humanly possible and brought back to life. He went from thirty-two pounds to nineteen pounds; he lost every hair on his body, including his eyebrows and lashes. He had fought and fought. He was the quarterback, and we had been his coaches.

The gray-haired doctor stood before me eighteen months later—eighteen torturous months later. My eighteen-month-old twins were asleep in their stroller, and Cannon was in the ICU, hooked up to machines that were pumping lifesaving immunotherapy into him.

The same doctor.

Not the same mother.

I began that eighteen-month journey as a mum of one,

The same doctor.
Not the same mother.

pregnant with twins, living in a different country, unsure of the medical landscape, and fearful that people wouldn't like me. Afraid I would upset doctors by getting second opinions, doctors who thought I should accept everything I was told and not question it.

Eighteen months later, that lassie was gone.

The, "I'm sorrys," and not asking questions or putting others' feelings first had disappeared.

The truth is, that lassie had to die for my son to live.

It was a case of either I die or he dies.

But, like tea bags, lassies, we never know how strong we are until we are in hot water.

Something inside me had changed. It was *no* longer just about questioning everything. It was to question it with excitement.

?

- What if he lives?
- What if we change the status quo of kids battling cancer by funding research?
- What if what we are doing helps hundreds of families?
- What if kids live because we do this work?

The excitement of hope changed everything for us.

> *The truth is, that lassie had to die*
> *for my son to live.*
> *It was a case of either I die or he dies.*
> *But, like tea bags, lassies, we never know*
> *how strong we are until we are in hot water.*

We no longer wanted to ask questions from fear, lack of hope, or despair.

My questions and my husband's questions led us there, eighteen months later, with a son still alive. Now he was age 3 and half, but he still couldn't talk. He'd lost his hearing from chemotherapy, he had scars on the outside, but most of the damage was on the inside. Unseen. What if we found a trial to change the trajectory of his life?

Cannon had a gene that meant his percentage for relapse of his cancer was very high. We were also told that, for Cannon, to relapse was to die. That led me to find this researcher in Michigan, Dr Giselle Scholar. She was doing an outside-the-box trial for kids like Cannon. It would require two more years of treatment, with the hope that his cancer would never return.

The gray-haired man said to me, "You're an absolute idiot if you do that trial." And he stormed out of our ICU room. He sent his nurse back later to apologize.

The same-old lassie would have chased him out the room, explained her point, and hoped he still liked her. Her desire to be liked and to please managed the show.

But the same lassie did not stand before him. She had changed.

She had chosen to *UnFollow Medical Gaslighting.*

She had chosen to *Follow* surgeons, hospitals, and trials with her husband by her side, and she knew her mind and trusted it. She knew the consequences of doing the opposite of what was suggested, and she did it anyway.

Cannon did go on the trial. That same trial was so successful, it is now part of the treatment for every child who has neuroblastoma. The once out-of-the-box trial is now mainstream and has saved hundreds of lives. It was so successful that, on October 4, 2023, the FDA voted, "Yes" to a trial drug. This was the first time in history the FDA relied on a single externally controlled trial approval in oncology.

It is difficult to put into words what this means in the cancer community, but without the work of Dr. Sholler and the advocacy of the non-profit Beat Childhood Cancer Foundation, this would not have happened. Had we, as a family, not questioned everything with excitement about our son living, he would not have been one of the first ten or so kids on this trial. Cannon signed the papers himself to document his progress, and he is one of the reasons why kids will have options today.

Maybe it is not medical gaslighting. Maybe it is someone else telling you what is right for you or calling you an idiot. No matter what it is, it ends *here*, with you picking up this book. Welcome to the world of *UnFollow, where we choose to follow Question Everything With Excitement.*

A year into our son's treatment, we used our learnings, of which there were many. We started Cannonball Kids' cancer Foundation, a nonprofit for research for kids with cancer. We have funded millions of dollars of research around the globe and in over half the states in the US.

Over eighty percent of our research is the first of its kind in the world. It's innovative and new, and more importantly, *it is not the same* hand-me-down adult treatments for kids. It has created over 700 clinical trial options for children around the world.

It is not the same. This is so key to its success.

Changing the status quo often means exactly that: change. Not staying the same.

One of our proudest moments was helping to fund the very trial that allowed me to keep our son alive, but at our local hospital, where that gray-haired doctor once worked.

I Knew.

You Also Know.

One of my favorite responses to my clients, when they say, "I don't know," is this:

"If you did know..., what would you do?"

The truth is, we all know. We know what we should do, the habits we should keep, the things we should say, and the areas in our life we need to question. Yet, ingrained consequences haunt us. Consequences like people calling us idiots, judging our choices, and pushing us to second guess ourselves.

This book is about questioning everything.

But more than that, it's about questioning everything with excitement! It's about questioning with an intention of hope, joy, and possibility, instead of fear, pain, and consequences.

It's about becoming your own life coach. It's about inner knowing. It's about relying less on outside chatter and believing more in the inside voice. When we question everything, and we do it with excitement and not shame or guilt, everything changes. If you want to win at your ONE.Life, start here.

Start by questioning everything with excitement.

This book is the reset for your ONE.Life. Inside and out, top to bottom.

Many of us are healing. In fact, I would go so far as to say all of us are, in some way. But are we all *living*. If we focus solely on healing and not on living, we miss out on the excitement and joy that is this ONE.Life.

Many of us are healing *but* are we living?

By living, we let go of perfectionism, parent- and people-pleasing, and decide to stop living on autopilot. We question diet cultures and body bullying, and we take steps toward self-responsibility. Together, we will question boundaries and divorce and everything in between. We will tackle martyrdom and work-life balance. Every roadblock you've ever had requires questions, and I plan to do just that with you.

Are you ready to question everything?

Then, you can decide what to *UnFollow*. Then and only then can you consciously choose what this version of you will *Follow*.

Let's begin! We have work to do.

?

> ❔
> ## THE WORK
> ### Follow Question
> ### Everything With Excitement

o   My intention word as I read this book is:
    What single word encapsulates what you hope to
    achieve or feel as you read through these pages?

o   As I read this book, I want to:
    Identify the transformation or insight you're seeking
    as you delve into this book.

o   The one thing in my life that will have the biggest
    impact by being questioned is:
    Is it a relationship, job, self-belief? What stands to gain
    the most from your thoughtful introspection?

o   What has been my autopilot mode and how has it
    served or hindered me?
    Examine the routines, habits, or belief systems you
    have unconsciously followed. Are they enhancing or
    limiting your life?

o   What are the goals I have set because someone else
    wanted them for me?
    Think about the ambitions you've chased to meet
    external expectations. Are they in line with your true
    self?

o   What am I most afraid to *UnFollow* and why?

❔

Explore the fears that anchor you to the familiar or to societal norms.

o Who is the person I'm pretending to be and how does that align with my authentic self?

Reflect on any "masks" you've worn to meet the expectations of others. How do these serve you, and what is the trade off?

o Who is my future self, what would thrill them the most about my life today?

Envision your future-self looking back. What would excite them about the choices and changes you're considering now?

o What is my favorite version of myself and what choices do I need to make to become that person?

Picture your favorite version of you. What steps can you take now to evolve into that version of you?

o What am I most excited to explore on this journey of introspection?

As you prepare to question everything with excitement, what specific queries spark your curiosity and eagerness?

o The one thing in my life that will have the biggest impact on being questioned is:

?

CHAPTER 2

UnFollow Self-Imposed Prisons

*"Lassies and lads, many of us are living
in self-imposed prisons, unaware that we ourselves
are both the prisoner and the guard."*

—Melissa Wiggins

You're here because you believe—perhaps on the surface, perhaps deep down—that something is missing. I believe that *something* is the rules and beliefs we have created for ourselves.

Have you ever been to jail? Me, neither. Okay that's a lie... Just once. I can confirm orange is *not* my color, and that I will never eat a bologna sandwich ever again.

OMG, OMG, Mum! I got it... I got it!! Dad! I got it!! I got the law internship in Orlando. I really got it!
You did not...
I did, too...
You did not...
I did! I did!!

My family is very excitable. We are that family that, if you marry into us, you absolutely will be doing a 5K on Turkey Day. Except not Turkey Day, as we are Scottish. So, maybe Haggis Day?

Let's go back.

I am the eldest of five kids.

People in my family didn't to go to college or law school or get internships in different countries. I am the lassie breaking glass ceilings, so you better put some shoes on. It was my last summer of internships in the U.S. I could not believe, when I got back, I would actually get to work as a trainee solicitor. This is a compulsory piece of becoming a solicitor (lawyer) in Scotland. I would finally get to wear my colored tights and cute suits and decorate my desk, *Legally Blonde*-style. It was finally here.

I don't want to undersell myself but I also don't want to oversell myself. I am not naturally smart. *Don't roll your eyes.* I set out to write a book as honestly as I am capable of, at this time. I am, however, a really hard worker, so I can learn and read and study anything. Literally. So, to be there... to be there... Oh, to be there. Bittersweet? What's that? I only tasted the sweet taste of victory!

The times I ate Christmas dinner and went straight to my desk, the times I said no to parties and holidays, the times my siblings teased me and said I was a geek, as all I did was study. *Bitter? Not in this hoose, pal.* (Please Google *Scottish slang* in conjunction with this book, to clarify any random Scottishness that comes oot me, when I get dead excited.)

Unlike most of my classmates, I worked three jobs throughout law school. That money paid for my flights to Orlando. I loved making my own money, and even though my parents did what they could for me, they had my younger siblings to take care of, and, frankly, my taste and their budget were not aligned. I blame my mum and my gran for these tastes of mine. Yes! I said *blame!* I take absolutely no responsibility for the development of these expensive tastes that they gave me.

I had a boyfriend in Orlando, so I stayed with him. We had been dating a few years. I loved him *a lot*, but I had zero plans to leave my career in Scotland and move Stateside. Not yet! I had been focused on this dream since the airing of the TV series, *Ally McBeal*, starring Calista Flockhart. She planted the seed in me to become a lawyer, and Reese Weatherspoon in *Legally Blonde* sealed the deal.

I wish that was a joke, but before you judge me, just remember, I was born in 1983. And did I mention I was from government housing and the first in my family to graduate high school and head to college? Anyway, there is so much more you can judge me on later, so best get comfy and put the kettle on, lassies and lads.

Reese Weatherspoon was completely underestimated by all the people, as was I. She was gorgeous; so was I. She was book smart; so was I. She was a fashion icon; so was I. The day was coming when I would drive up to my first job in my... well, actually, more like walking on my legs, since I didn't have a car and, well, everyone walks in Edinburgh, but with my box of pink office supplies. I mean, did I send a résumé in pink scented paper? And did I get the job?

True story. They knew who I was, and they would love me. They did love me. My interviews, all three stages of them, were killer. I had them laughing and forgetting about my odd C grade before they knew it. The job was mine, and sweet it would be. A two-year contract, and I would get to go to court and stand before a judge and represent clients. Yes, I would. All sweet... No bitter.

At age twenty-three and heading back to Scotland to work at the best real estate litigation firm in my home country—it all awaited me. This would be my summer. This one.

Oh sweet, Florida... I love you! You're sunny every day! Your blue skies are beyond, have nothing but white clouds, and your sunsets are the scenes of every romantic movie. Scotland is gray and gray and gray and more gray. Six months of the year, we go to work in the dark and come home in the dark. To be clear, I can say this: I am Scottish. *You* cannot say this. You must only say how incredible my country is and how brilliant your trip was, unless, of course, you're also Scottish. Then, you can do whatever the heck you want, because you're likely a little scary.

"Reporting for duty," I said in a weirdly perky voice to the lady at the front desk.

"Sorry...?"

The joke didn't land... Cough, cough....

"Melissa Gray. I was told to be here at 9:00 a.m. to start my internship."

"The Scottish girl, yes?"

I don't know why, but I *hate* when people call me a girl. I was twenty-three, not a thirteen-year-old. I allowed my initial irritation at her tone to pass and smiled as big as Elle Woods *(Legally Blonde)* on her first day. I pushed down my thoughts around worthiness and the loud noises inside me that wanted to yell, "*I am smart! I am smart!*"

I followed her to a windowless room, where she showed me the files that she had placed out for me.

"I need you to go through each of these and do summary reports for the attorney."

Right away, I was excited. I am a nerd. I didn't let the windowless room or the yucky brown folder color take my joy; instead, I got to work. I, of course, worked longer than I should and showed up before I should because..., well, I am me and that is what I do.

"Hey, Friday, 5:00 p.m., we are going for happy hour drinks. Want to come?"

I looked around. Yup, this invite was definitely directed at me. No one else was in this windowless room. No other interns, like at my previous jobs.

In my perky, weird voice, I said, "Yes! I would love that!"

I reminded my brain not to follow up with any more verbiage. *They don't need the 500-word summary of how you have no friends in America or how alcohol is the boss of your life and you have no idea how to stop that, despite trying every day, despite making false promises to yourself.*

Most of us live in prisons, ones we've created. It is a bondage to self that runs so deep, we can't even see where the root started. We sit in the comfort of the known jail cell. It's safe here. We know what's in here, and nothing goes in or out without us seeing it. We live in the cozy comfort of that prison. Opinions don't hurt us here. Fear is our master and our protector, in this codependent nightmare.

Alcohol was my boss at twenty-three. I was what people would call a high-functioning alcoholic! Definition: a lassie or lad who doesn't live under a bridge and has a job. *(You really need to buy the audio to hear me say that.)*

In fact, she had been my master for quite some time.

Like most high-functioning alcoholics, I had zero desire to ever stop this relationship with her. She was my best friend. She had never let me down; she would never, or could never leave me—like ever.

She is a bottle of red wine—the finest kind, of course, from the finest vineyard. After a hard day of law school, she was always there, waiting for me. She never didn't show. *Pop!* The noise of her cork coming out. A sigh... A deep breath, knowing that I was okay now. Truly okay. The first few drops of her into a beautiful glass. Her color, her smell—God, she is everything!

That first taste... and all the anxiety slipped away. The hard class, the part-time jobs, the wondering if Kimberley from litigation class was talking about me as I walked into the room, the thoughts about why I didn't get invited into the study group like last time... All gone. Nothing to worry about. A few more sips, another bottle, and three more episodes of *Grey's Anatomy,* and I never wanted friends anyway. Who even cares if Lauren likes me...? *Witch.* Study groups are for losers, and I will get an A grade alone, thank you very much, you bunch of codependent losers.

Eyes open...

Panic.

Where am I?

Okay, I'm home. I'm okay. I'm in my same clothes. Crap, what time is it? OMG, I've got to get to class. Shower? Do I have time? No. Darn it.

?

*More panic. OMG, dare I look at my texts and calls? Please,
do not have called or texted anyone, especially not Lauren or
anyone in the study group. Please, God no. I will never drink
again if there are no calls or texts.*
OMG, No Calls!
Okay, time for class.
I am never drinking again. It is not worth it.
This feeling of panic and nausea was unbearable. I stayed
in the library late, so as not to go home and drink. It worked.
Yes, I didn't drink. This was amazing. I could totally not drink,
if I chose. It was my choice. I was in charge of my life, and I
said, "No."

Two days would pass, maybe three. I was convinced: I
totally do not have a problem with alcohol. It's just stress from
school.

"You waaaant any cris wae yer wine, hen?" (translation:
"Do you want any chips with your wine, hun?")

"Sure, the jalapeno, thanks."

And so, the story continued...

Never again... Again.

Never, never, never again...... Again.

There I was, in the U.S. on my internship, being invited for
happy hour drinks.

"So, should we just get taxis? Or how are you all getting
there?"

"Oh, everyone just drives, just for a few at happy hour!"

Most of that night was a complete blackout for me.

This is where my drinking was at twenty-three.
Sometimes, I could have one and go home. Sometimes, I
blacked out and woke up... *Panic. Where am I?*

That night, I recall being in my car, a black VW Beetle.
When I drank, like many people, I felt more confident, like
nothing could touch me.

No one was on the road. I put my foot all the way down to
the floor. The wheel was shaking. I wondered if I would die. It

?

didn't matter, I thought. Then, I thought, *Is that normal?* Do all people think that? What's normal anyway?

In this moment, none of my loved ones were in my brain, not my boyfriend, not my parents or siblings. This prison was me, the road, and a very shaky wheel.

I released the pedal, slowed down, and then I sped up again. This time, I was not so lucky. The car hit the center median and rolled and rolled and rolled and rolled. I was upside down. My seatbelt was on, and I was hanging upside down.

A light flashed in my eyes. I couldn't see. I unbuckled myself and fell to the roof of the car. Then, I pushed the car door open and slid out.

A man was yelling, "Is she okay? Is she okay?"

I pushed my hands off the grass... I was on grass...! And slid back from the car. The car was in a ditch of grass on the side of the highway.

"Are you hurt?" asked the man. The man was a state trooper.

"No, no, I don't feel hurt. I don't think so?" My brain asked how can I not be hurt after rolling my car four times and getting out upside down?

"Do you need an ambulance?" says the trooper in a deep voice. He wasn't unfriendly, but he wasn't friendly either. He was serious. Not unkind, but not kind.

"Have you been drinking?"

I would need to do a sobriety test. Of course, I miserably failed said test, and I was handcuffed. *Handcuffed*! *YES! HANDCUFFED!*

At this point of writing the book, I seriously considered deleting the entire chapter and writing some meek, low-key story about how I woke up once after drinking with bruises on me and how that made me say, "Oh, you should probably stop this nonsense, sweet girl," and that's all it took. I stopped. End of chapter.

My goal for my ONE.Life is, if sharing these stories helps one person change their life, then it was all worth it to me. Even if it requires very uncomfortable conversations with the most important people in my life.

The man with the deep voice put me in the back of his car. There was a glass between us, and the seat was not a normal seat. It was hard. It reminded me of the bus I would sometimes take to law school in Edinburgh. And then, I did what every twenty-three-year-old would do in my position when they realize they just screwed up their whole life. Yes, you guessed it, I started bawling.

I told the man with the deep voice that I just graduated law school, and that I would start my first job at the end of the summer.

"Will I still be able to practice law with this?" I asked, as if the man with the deep voice knew my future.

This time, he spoke to me in a different voice, a softer voice. "You will still be able to be a lawyer."

I gasped... I was wrong. He was kind, he was nice.

I was placed in a small cell with other women. Still feeling "oh, so powerful" from my intoxication, I didn't let them scare me. I stood tall and made eye contact. If only they knew, as soon as this wears off, I would be a ball in the corner; but they didn't, so I remained okay.

I was moved into a larger cell, with bunks and around twenty other lassies. I picked a bottom bunk and pulled up the scratchy blanket over me. I didn't dare sleep, as by then my bravery had fully worn off, and let's just say it was best to keep one eye open that night. The reality of the situation was hitting me.

At intake, I was able to call my boyfriend. He was a lawyer and able to bail me out of jail the next morning. The pain in his face as he picked me up is a look I won't ever forget, and that's a good thing. I was horrified, he was horrified. It was a living nightmare.

The car ride back to his house was quiet, painful. He was thankful I was alive but had questions. We got into his bed, and I was so very sore. My whole body hurt. We turned on the TV, and there it was, the end of my life, *on TV*. I started to recall there had been a TV van and camera at the scene.

"Scottish lawyer arrested for drunk driving on I-4, the young twenty-three-year-old is here on an internship with a local law firm..."

"Turn it off. Turn it off."

I wasn't ready.

I simply wasn't ready.

But I would be.

A white plastic chair awaited me...

Alcohol was my self-imposed prison. I placed myself there. I liked it. I knew her, and she was always there, but she was no longer safe. I couldn't trust her anymore. I was not free, but freedom felt unsafe. Like the boat that stays at harbor, I was safe; but to go out from shore, to the unknown—how could that be freedom?

So, I did the next logical thing. I stopped drinking around people. That was my master plan. The plan that would ensure I would never, ever again be on TV for drinking. This way, I would be safe. *She* is safe. *We* are safe. I would drink at home and alone!

This is where I see all problem drinkers end up: lonely, isolated, and afraid on the inside. On the outside, we live big, brilliant, amazeballs lives. We talk on stages and host top-rated podcasts. We are judges and nuns and lawyers, and we are dead inside.

I returned home to Scotland, remorseful but in complete denial that stopping drinking would end my misery. My first night home in Scotland, my dad handed me a beer. My three months of non-drinking felt like penance enough. I wasn't ready for the white plastic chair yet, I wasn't done yet, but I would be...

Maybe it's not alcohol for you. Maybe your self-imposed prison is binge eating or pain pills. Maybe it's not as dramatic as that, and it's simply that fear rules you, and you allow it. Maybe it's that you can't set boundaries with your family, so you live for them, not with them. Maybe it's a relationship.

Don't overthink this. Hello, fellow overthinker. I see you trying to skip *The Work*.

I want you to question everything with excitement.

❗

THE WORK

Follow Freedom

---

o   What would a morning feel like waking up sober?

o   What would a day not consumed by fear of whether I will black out look like?

o   What would I do with my time and energy, if it wasn't consumed by my obsession with alcohol?

When you question from there, instead of out of fear and shame about how you got here or why you can't stop or believe you are just like your family, you can't move forward with the same momentum.

Instead, close your eyes:

o   What is the first thing that comes into your wee noggin? What prison have you imposed on yourself?

o   What if, today, you told one other person that?

Shame cannot live in the light, sweet friend. I have never publicly told the story of being arrested, never shared it on social media, and because of this book and the value I feel this story will bring, I had to tell my children about this before we published it.

I had to show them that I made mistakes, that perfectionism is against our religion in this home, and how, instead, we strive for knowing ourselves and becoming our favorite version of ourselves. Thank you to Melissa Parsons, who was the first person I ever heard talk about favorite version over best self. My life has never been the same.

o Does your favorite version of yourself do this thing?

o What would your favorite version of yourself tell you?

o Write down everything amazeballs that will happen in your ONE.Life, if you take yourself out of this self-imposed prison and you are free to be that favorite version of yourself.

o Who can help you?

o Who will support this shift in you?

o Tell that person you want their help. This will change your life from the inside out.

CHAPTER 3

UnFollow Blame

"The price of greatness is responsibility."
—Winston Churchill

"Hello......"
"*Hi, you have reached the Hotline. How can I help you?*"
I hung up.

It was Sunday morning. I woke up with my female friend from work in my bed and bruises all over my body.

"Are you okay?" she softly whispered.

In my usual way, I said, "Of course I am. Why wouldn't I be?" My method, when I don't recall how I acted or how much I drank, was always to act like everything was fine. Where is that metaphorical rug? Let me sweep everything under you. Lumpy..., but, we good.

"Babe, you fell down the stairs, and your neighbor was going to call the police. You kept saying that was your flat and it wasn't. You scared me."

This was a particularly bad night for me. As you may recall, I don't drink with other people anymore, but for some reason, I took the bait and joined the other lawyers from my firm for after-work drinks.

I called again.

"*Hi.*"

"Hi."

"*Is alcohol your best friend?*" said a strong voice on the other end.

"*Ummmmm, noooo.* Of course not. That's stupid."

"Really?"

"Yes. Really."

I was feeling a little annoyed by her harsh tone, but for some reason (despair?), I stayed on the line.

"Well, do you care about her more than anything else?"

Again, "No. I am a lawyer. I work. I care about lots of things."

"But you care more about drinking and not giving her up, don't you?"

Who the heck does this lassie think she is? I wondered. She doesn't know me, she's never even met me.

"Don't drink tonight or tomorrow. I will pick you up after work and take you to a meeting."

"Oh, I don't need a meeting. I just..."

"You just, what?"

"Well, last night was hard. I have a lot of stress, and I drink like everyone else I know."

"Pick you up at 6 p.m. Don't drink!"

The line went dead.

My stomach... *OMG, I'm going to puke.*

I was twenty-five. I was always first in the office and last out. It was 7 a.m. on Monday. All day, I was nervous. Maybe, I wouldn't go home, so then she couldn't take me. But then, I found myself walking home. I found myself leaving my desk much earlier than normal, so as not to be late.

The nausea didn't subside all day. I got home and changed out of my red-colored tights (stockings) and gray pencil skirt, crisp, white shirt, and matching blazer. I thought, *What can I wear that is subtle?*

I looked in my closet. I didn't own subtle clothes. Try and find something black in my closet... I dare you! You can't. So, I was screwed. White, oversized jumper and jean trousers.

I peeked out my flat windows. They were floor-to-ceiling in this old, 1880s Victorian building, so being subtle was impossible.

Maybe she won't come, I thought.

Best friend? I mean, really?

The flat buzzer went off. I jumped. She was pushing the buzzer. I pressed the button inside my flat

"Yessss," I said, softly.

"It's me, Sheri. For the meeting, from the hotline. You ready?"

Was I ready? Ready for what? For you to take my joy? Probably some cult, anyway. Was I ready? Of course, these are all thoughts. I responded, "Yup, coming down."

I got in her tiny, white, two-door car. Maybe she wasn't really someone who answered the call, but was pretending to be and really planned to murder me. I'd told no one of my whereabouts—what would I even have said?

"Oh, hi, Mum. Just to let you know I'm headed to break up with my best friend. Here is the location. Oh well, this is the end. I've had twenty-five good years."

"So, did you drink today?" she asked as we drove.

I smirked. *Didn't I tell you, I'm a lawyer? I work. Like all day, every day. So, no.*

I thought, *Drink at work? Puh-leeeze. I have some self-respect. I wait until I am home alone and no one is around to drink myself into oblivion.'*

"No...," I said softly, picking my nails and staring at the floor of the car, while praying not to be murdered.

"Great! You will love this meeting. Such amazing people...."

Suddenly, I knew she was talking, but I couldn't hear the words. I had totally dissociated.

Suddenly, it dawned on me. *What if someone sees me? What if someone from my firm is there, like one of the partners or paralegals?* My life would be over.

My life *was* over.

We parked—you guessed it—outside a church. We walked downstairs—you guessed it—to a basement. The clichés were outstanding.

I only knew this from American TV. I never knew anyone growing up who got sober. I knew a lot of not sober people.

Drinking a lot in my country was kind of part of the deal, and sobriety was for the weak. I was *not* weak, so how did I get there? I was not weak. I'd never cried a day in my life. *Ohhh... Maybe... No...*

We walked in and, of course, everyone knew Sheri, and Sheri knew everyone, so there I was, trying to be subtle in my non-subtle clothes and trying to be polite. But also, what in the actual world?

"Tea?" someone said, while nudging a cup at me that looked freshly made. "Biscuit?"

"No. No, thank you." Tea and biscuit... There had to be a hidden camera there. What was this, social hour?

Sheri said to go take a seat, and I walked into the other room. Chair after chair after chair. *Good grief, how many of them are there?*

The room was set up in such a manner that there was zero, and I mean *zero* way not to be spotted or spoken to. But I don't give up easily. I put my hands under my jean trousers and my head down, and I stared at the floor. It was wood. We were in a church basement. It smelled like church, musty but comforting.

Everyone nestled in, and it got noisy. These lassies and lads could gab. Weren't they exhausted from work? *Do they work?* I wondered, judging with my judgy brain.

"All Right, everyone. Who's ready for a meeting?" an older man said in a very chippy voice, like Santa-Claus chippy.

Everyone chuckled and said, "Yes."

Wait! *Are these people happy?* Like actually happy to be sitting on a white plastic chair in a basement of a musty church, instead of being home after work?

It didn't matter anyway. I would not be back. One meeting for Sheri, to prove that alcohol was not my friend, and goodbye. These people were so much older than me, anyway.

I did not look up from the floor once. The terror of seeing someone I knew prevented me. That is, until I heard these words: "Hi, I'm Leslie. I'm an alcoholic, and I love this meeting topic."

She sounded young. I looked up. She *was* young, maybe my age, maybe a few years older. She sounded happy.

"I cannot believe I am five years sober. The gifts of sobriety have changed my life. This weekend, I went out with lots of friends and my boyfriend, and everyone drank but I didn't. But I had so much fun. *So* much fun, guys. We laughed and danced, and the next day, when they were hungover, I went for a run."

My brain thought: *Sure. That can't be true. No way. How? Can you? Could you? Did she?*

Could I?

Prior to that moment, I'd believed with my entire being that there was zero way to dance, have fun, or laugh without a little alcohol in one's system. I was very fun, but it required wine to get there.

Leslie made a beeline for me at the end of the meeting.

"I would love to take you for a cup of tea."

That cup of tea changed my life. Maybe that's why I called my podcast, *Coaching and A Cup of Tea with Mummabear*.

Leslie changed my life. That meeting. That share. That basement. The white plastic chair. The musty church smell. All of it. Changed my whole life.

I haven't drank alcohol since that cup of tea with Leslie, more than fourteen years ago.

Like most addicts, whether it's sex, money, drugs, alcohol, shopping—we are the worst. I speak for all of us. Okay, fine. I will speak for me. *I* was the worst. *The worst.*

I was the alcoholic who didn't show up for the dinner you made from scratch. I was the one who borrowed your dress, got a stain on it, and called you a not-so-nice name for being mad about it—behind your back, of course. I was the lassie who was shunned from study groups in two colleges in two degrees and cried to my mum, "Why don't girls like me?" I was the worst. I took zero responsibility for my life and blamed everyone around me. I was the original victim, in victim mentality.

I recall, in early sobriety, Leslie asked me whom I'd hurt when drinking. My denial was so deep, I responded, "Mostly myself."

Good Lord, slap that lassie in the face. But Leslie didn't. She smiled and stayed the course. The course of showing up. The course of helping me to become a better friend, a better daughter. The course where selfishness is eroded away at the soul and problems are ripped out by their roots. The course where the only requirement for a new way of living is a simple desire to not want to drink. Leslie stayed the course.

The first year of sobriety was both terrifying and liberating. It was in equal parts a shock to my core and a steadying of my soul.

I told no one. After the shame disappeared and I saw my insides change, I wanted to make sure no one convinced me to stop. I feared this. I had been a people-pleaser my whole life, and the thought of my family, my boyfriend, or anyone thinking I was not an alcoholic scared me. When I talked to my priest about my drinking, he held my hand and said, "Dear, you are not an alcoholic. You are just having a hard time." Case in point.

But I knew. The soft callings of my soul told me: "You are, and it's okay."

It wasn't okay.

But it became okay.

And I am okay. The option to become the worst again is out there, too. It's available for me, should I take a drink, and you would know, because I would never be okay.

> *"The best years of your life are the ones in which you decide*
> *your problems are your own. You do not blame them on*
> *your mother, the ecology, or the president.*
> *You realize that you control your own destiny."*
> —Albert Ellis

THE WORK

Follow I am Responsible

I didn't decide to be responsible for my ONE.Life. I became responsible, one action at a time. It's not a decision, but a doing.

I have chosen for over fourteen years to show up for meetings, to have hotline parties, answer the phone, and to pick up newcomers, like Sheri did for me. I have chosen to go on retreats, to call my sponsor, and to be a sponsor. It's action.

It was my thought to call the hotline. It was my decision to get in Sheri's car.

o   What are you thinking about now?

o   Who are you blaming?

o   What are you blaming?

Maybe you had a rough childhood. Maybe you were abused. Maybe you lost a parent young. Maybe it is none of those, and yet you still know there is more to this ONE.Life. Maybe the victim mentality was taught or learned, and maybe it was neither. And yet here you are.

o   List areas of your life you are responsible for:

o   List areas you wish you were, and ways you can

change that reality:

o   What action can you take today? This is not, I repeat
    not a thought prompt. This is a *do* prompt.

o   What can you do today to stop blaming and start
    doing?

Are you terrified? Good. Do it with nausea and butterflies.
Be so close to not doing it, but do it anyway.

When my clients join my six-month coaching intensive,
EMPOWERED.Life, we start here. They are not addicted to
drugs, alcohol, sex, or money. Often, they are addicted to
pleasing people, to perfectionism, to busyness—things that
are quite literally as deadly as my addiction.

Often, they blame the kids' sports schedules and their
family for stepping on their boundaries. They claim it's
because they have the job they have and they can't change.
They tell me they were born in a certain state and they cannot
"just move."

What if all that changed just by taking some actions of
responsibility and not blaming your kids and parents or
bowing down to every societal norm we have been fed?

o   What is *one* action you can do today, and for the next
    seven days, you can repeat it without fail?

o   If *one* action could change your ONE.Life in a positive
    way, what would it be?

As you begin to answer these questions, do it with the
cloud of excitement over you. With the hope and joy of what
self-responsibility can mean in your life. What can choosing to
UnFollow blame do for you, in the most exciting way.

Choosing to *Follow*, I am responsible is exciting. It's
freedom. It's joy. It's possibility. It's letting go and forgiving, so
you can have the ONE.Life you desire.

?

CHAPTER 4

UnFollow Lassies who Lunch

*"There is no passion to be found playing small and settling for
a life that is less than the one you are capable of living."*
—Nelson Mandela

Unfollowing is choosing nature over nightclubs, healing over hustling, energy over economics, and, well, walking over lunching.

Kelly: "Does June third work?"

Me: "No, I'm out of town."

Kelly: "What about July eighteenth?"

Me: "Kids have camp that week, and Michael is out of town. What about the week after?"

Sound familiar? When adulting and adult friendships feel like a game of tag where there is no winner, it's time to UnFollow. UnFollow the lassies who lunch; frankly, lunches feel like I'm losing. Seventeen exhausting texts later, I get something on my calendar, only to spend $40 on some average lunch and just as much on babysitting, to make it happen.

The same week, two of my good friends report the hardship of adult female relationships. I see my friend Sam Joy host a walking group. I think, "I love walking." I walk every day, and once a week, my girl Lourdes and I walk and talk for an hour. Lives are saved in that hour—you are welcome.

I challenge my clients to do walk-and-talks with me during our one-on-one sessions. I wrote a lot of this book and the ideas behind it on my walks. Walking has to be one of the single most underrated forms of exercise known to man.

While I'm on the phone with Sam Joy, she says, "Do it! Have your own walking group."

So, I do what most of us do when we have ideas: I go straight to Canva to create a flyer. This flyer will be posted on my social media and I will call the group, "Women Who Walk, Win."

You see, walking feels like winning. I'm moving. I'm outside. I'm in community—did I mention, real lives were saved during my walks with Lourdes? You, too, can save lives. Create your own walking group.

I love the concept of two birds, one stone. So, my group is a "bring your friend" group. Let's together UnFollow the seventeen-text method only for no dates to work. Let's UnFollow the expensive, average-tasting lunches and meet our friends every week together at the same time, same day, and same place.

Since starting this group, when lassies have asked to meet me, I've given them the date, time, and location, and, of course, my cute Canva, and I've said, "Let's walk for an hour."

I've seen more friends and laughed more and felt more connected than I have in years. We lassies—okay, me—we overcomplicate things. We often don't question the societal norms, and if we do question them, it's certainly not from a place of excitement.

UnFollowing social or societal life norms like ladies must meet for lunch, and saying, "No, thanks. I'd rather Follow women who walk, win."

Our group will meet every week without fail, thanks to a few amazeballs friends who host the walk when I travel.

Heidi is my friend and client, and I've seen her at every walk. This makes my heart smile so big. I hadn't seen her in six months prior to walk club.

One very long and not-awkward hug later, she said, "You will be so proud of me." She said this with such joy in her voice, tucking her beautiful blonde hair behind an ear and smiling so big at me.

Her smile is infectious, and I smiled so big back. It was 7:00 a.m. on a Monday morning, and there were no Monday blues there, only the sun rising over the lake and chitter-chatter in front and behind us. I heard giggles way back, and I quickly looked around to see two old friends laughing. My heart. This moment. Outside. Walking. Being present and laughing. "Holy heaven, lassie," I thought to myself. "This is living. This."

"Well, I am always proud of you, lassie, but tell me all the things."

Heidi came to me feeling broken, a self-proclaimed workaholic, and, despite her massive success as a top producer in her company, she felt lost and helpless.

A message popped up in my messenger: "*I need your help. Someone suggested you.*"

We exchanged numbers and I drove my minivan, aka my portable office, to the lake. I dialed the number.

"*Melissa.*"

"Hi, Heidi. Everything okay?"

"*No. No, it's not. Something awful has happened on social media, and I'm being bashed, and I didn't mean it, and—*"

"Heidi. Heidi. Let's meet."

The next day, we met at the Glass Knife, a cute little pink bakery in Winter Park, Florida. We sat outside, because it was busy.

Heidi vomited everything out she needed to, and then said, "When can we start?"

"What do you want, Heidi?"

"I want to be present, but I don't know how. I want to get off this hamster wheel of non-stop achieving. I want my kids to get in my car and me not be on a work call, asking them to hush until I'm finished. I want... Well, I want to enjoy my life. I want to enjoy my core four. My family. I want there to be more to me than, 'I'm great at my job.' I want my daughter to come to me and share her life."

"So, let's start there."

Twelve months of coaching and two retreats at The Magical Lakehouse later, Heidi said, "You will be so proud of me. I did something I've never done before."

I couldn't wait to hear. Such anticipation.

"I booked a two-week vacation to one of the world's seven Blue Zones with my family."

I coach high performance people. Heidi is as HP as they come. But I don't coach them to get further up in their company, which, for Heidi, would be impossible, since, hello, she was already there. Instead, I coach them to deeply enjoy the fruits of their labor and how to be healed from the high-performance perfectionism that can manifest as we climb the ladder.

Heidi looked so proud. She said, "There is more. I just got off a quality-time staycation with my four, just us four. Time spent with intention and reconnection. We swam, we cruised the lazy river 400 times, and my girl and I snuggled up to *Survivor* and had deep conversations."

People like Heidi don't need productivity hacks or energy hacks. They have mastered work. They are the CEOs of their work. They love work. The problem is work doesn't love you back.

Guess what? Heidi is just as successful in her work now as she was when we first met. The only difference now is, she knows how to switch her phone and her brain off autopilot and be present with people she loves. Heidi needed to learn to trust herself—trust that she could rest and be present without losing everything she'd worked for. With deep trust in self comes deep love, and with deep love comes an ability to shut off parts of your brain and be present.

Heidi's son's teacher called her and said he was different. Something had shifted. And he'd told his teacher his mum had a coach. The truth was, Heidi wanted change. She didn't know how to get it, but she knew she wanted it, and that's where the magic happens.

Heidi was lost in the forest; she couldn't see the path. Coaching was her drone, her way of floating above the forest and seeing everything in plain sight. Seeing the right path for her marriage and her kids and her ONE.Life.

Heidi will tell you that I changed her life. She will stand tall and tell anyone this fact. But the true fact is, Heidi changed my life. I was a new coach when she found me, I had just earned my master certification, and she believed in me. Her belief in me is one of the many reasons she changed my life.

I say it all the time: I am the luckiest. Every day, when a lassie or lad invites me into their life and bares their soul to me, I think, again and again, *I am the luckiest.* This book is for many people, but much of it is written for the beautiful Heidis of the world.

❕

THE WORK

Follow Women Who Walk Win

Does a "Women Who Walk, Win" group feel exciting for you? If not, what does? Weekly book club? Weekly yoga in the park? Decide, and then do it. Ask yourself these questions from a place of excitement. Imagine if, weekly, you connected with your friends. Imagine if you were capable of high achieving and enjoyed rest. Imagine if you could be present with your people and not always thinking about work.

o   Are you a Heidi?

o   Do you have success and yet struggle to enjoy it?
    Like Heidi, list the things you want. It's an exercise in awareness of what you don't want.

o   Right now, go into your phone, and set three daily alarms, every day at the same time and name them "Presence, Pause."
    When the alarms go off, set a one-minute timer. In that time, get present. Look at where you are, what's around you, and touch the surface around you. What do you see, smell, feel? This exercise will start to change your ability to be present.

o Set a reminder on your phone. Mine is 9:00 p.m., and it says, "Time to unwind, beautiful lassie." What will yours say? What time will you set it?

My phone is placed in another room at that point, and it's my signal to my body to get ready for bed.

o Commit to moving your body for thirty minutes every day. If you do six days and the seventh day you don't show up for yourself, start again.

I love to walk but also love the gym, yoga, biking, surfing, and hiking. What is your favorite way to move your body? You do not need to commit to sixty- and ninety-minute workouts to get the benefits. Research in this area is very conclusive: thirty minutes of movement is all you need for overall health and wellbeing.

Heidi committed to yoga. Why? She loves it. Stop doing all the movement you think you need, and instead mix it up. Keep it fun and enjoyable. If thirty minutes feels overwhelming, do what I did. I started at ten minutes a day and built up to what felt empowering.

Remember, this work is about choosing to *UnFollow* everything you have been taught and choosing to *Follow* what feels empowering to your ONE.Life. Movement is medicine. Let it be.

"Trust yourself. Create the kind of self
that you will be happy to live with all your life."
—Golda Meir

o What could prevent me from growing my trust in myself?
Identify the barriers, both internal and external, that may be hindering your self-trust. Is it past failures, fear of judgement, or perhaps lack of self-awareness?

o What past experiences have eroded my trust in myself?
Reflect on specific instances where your self-trust took a hit. How have these experiences shaped your current level of self-trust?

o What affirmations or mantras can you use to reinforce trust in yourself?
Craft empowering statements that you can repeat to yourself in moments of doubt. What words resonate with you on this journey?

o When have you successfully trusted your instincts and what was the outcome?
Recall instances where trusting yourself led to positive results. How can you apply those lessons to future situations?

o What activities or practices make you feel most in touch with your inner wisdom?
Identify actions or routines that help you tune into your inner voice. How can you incorporate these into your daily life?

o What role do external influences (friends, family, media) play in your level of self-trust?
Examine the impact of outside voices on your ability to trust yourself. Are they bolstering your self-trust or undermining it?

○ How can you measure the growth of yourself over time?

Consider benchmarks or signs that will indicate you are growing self-trust. Is it taking more risks, seeking less external validation, or something else?

CHAPTER 5

UnFollow Autopilot

"If you can't explain it simply,
you don't understand it well enough."
—Albert Einstein

"Until you make the unconscious conscious,
it will direct your life and you will call it Fate."
—Carl Jung

Consciousness seems so fancy and elusive to me, after reading some forty books on the topic (out of hundreds of thousands, it seems; perhaps a slight exaggeration, but, hello, I'm Scottish, as we talked about already!). My goal of reading this not-easy-to-read literature was to do what I do best, my literal superpower: *make the complicated simple.*

Frankly, in my experience, my people don't want to consume these books; they want the actionable tool. So, here's to living the words of Albert Einstein and explaining consciousness so simply, you won't ever need to read any of the books I did. I am never getting that time back, lassies and lads.

Oh, Europe, you are just so yummy. Truly—the feeling of being back in the past, at a slower time, is pretty magical. While I loved Barcelona and Madrid, my heart really fell in love with Valencia, a seaside town that actually invented the paella dish.

?

Hubby and I were about to meet our guide, Ramon, and visit the market to buy everything we needed to make paella. He walked us through it, step-by-step, and we participated in every aspect of it.

Afterward, as I sat beside my husband, chatting to six other couples who were also on this adventure, I almost forgot I was six days into a ten-day challenge of having my phone on airplane mode. I smiled. *Yes. This is living,* I thought. Then, I gasped, realizing I'd had no anxiety this whole trip.

Hello, my fellow anxious people. The realization of my lack of anxiety and my phone being on airplane mode didn't surprise me. You see, a big part of consciousness is being where your feet are.

Consciousness, simply put, is your brain on airplane mode. It is the awareness of one's thoughts, feelings, and surroundings It is being truly awake for this ONE.Life.

Airplane mode allows you to take in what's in front of you. Think about airplane mode—there are fewer distractions, more space for clarity and filtering out external noise. It allows your phone to be in a state of rest, just like consciousness allows you to be here now—where your feet are. This mode saves your phone battery—just like consciousness saves your mental energy. It allows you to focus your mental energy in a direction on purpose. Turning on airplane mode is a conscious choice to disconnect, just like being conscious is a choice to engage deeply with everything in your ONE.Life.

For example, my entire experience as a result of having my phone on airplane mode in the market while selecting the chicken we bought for the paella. The connection I felt as I attempted to speak Spanish (horribly, I might add), as we purchased the ingredients. The aroma of the rice as it settled in and boiled on the large, flat pan. Consciousness when laughing and feeling the *joy* inside me, as we all congratulated ourselves on our great cooking. A life without distraction. A mode where you are where your feet are. Where the only people who have access to you are with you.

You notice everything, from smells to touch to taste. No one has to repeat a sentence to you, because, well, you're looking them in the eyes, taking in their every word. Time slows down. A mode where you are awake.

Almost every client I've ever had the honor of working with has struggled with being present. How can we make the unconscious conscious, as Carl Jung puts it, if we don't even know how to be conscious? Like most things in life, we have overcomplicated consciousness.

If someone had told me, "Coach Mummabear, autopilot is how you feel when your phone is on, and being conscious is more how you feel when your phone is on airplane mode," I would have greatly appreciated it. So, you're welcome!

I am all about self-responsibility; *me* responsible is my jam. But, lassies and lads, we have got to make the unconscious conscious to even be in the game of life.

When our phones are on regular mode, notifications are checked. Calls are answered. Texts are responded to immediately. We become these reactive beings who couldn't live in the present moment even if we tried. Since ninety-five percent of what we do is run by our subconscious, just doing what it is programmed to do and we are used to doing, we live in autopilot.

Autopilot is the exact opposite of airplane mode. It's being addicted to the busy and fast, terrified of the present moment and slow. Yes, terrified. Our addiction to busy keeps us in autopilot, and our fear of slowing down prevents us from moving out of it.

One client told me she feels like she is on a hamster wheel with no idea of how to step off. One client cried as she handed me her phone for three days, while at a retreat I hosted.

Our phones have become the boss of us. Unknowingly, we have signed these subconscious contracts that say, "I am available 24/7. Your emergency is my emergency. And anytime you text, I will write you back."

Our phones are like the bully who, for some reason, we just wish they liked us, but they never will; instead, they use us and reward us with dopamine every time we slide, like, comment, or respond. Dopamine is the same chemical released when we eat or have sex. Our brain is designed to release it when we do something that meets survival needs.

Now, studies are showing that, when we use our phones, the same thing happens. The problem is that very dopamine reward loop—pick up your phone and your brain sends a reward to you. Your dopamine increases, you feel happy, but then shortly afterward, the dopamine decreases, so we pick up the phone again.

Is it any surprise that my clients struggle to hand me their phone on retreats? That they often cry and start giving me six to seven good reasons why they should keep it in their room. Look at what we mere mortals are up against:

The average American checks their phone 144 times a day, essentially every ten minutes. Eighty-nine percent of Americans check their phone within ten minutes of waking up. Seventy percent of us use our phone on the toilet. Sixty percent of us sleep with it at night. Seventy-five percent of us check our phone within five minutes of notifications. (Source: reviews.org).

Screen time has risen thirty percent in the last year, with the average American spending four and a half hours on screen time. Eighty-two percent of us said we would take our phones, if there was a house fire.

Ten days of having my phone on airplane mode is something I have committed to every year. My husband's phone is on for emergencies, and I am finally able to be the boss of my own life. I wake up and start my mornings not checking my phone. I don't have seventy-seven notifications from Instagram, and there is no one to text or respond to. My anxiety isn't through the roof, because I'm frantically following a missing submarine story or an awful situation at our borders. I am there—cooking paella, laughing, feeling, and I am where my feet are. I am awake. I am, simply put, conscious. Autopilot can't live here.

Shortly after one of my retreats, in our group chat, one attendee said, "But how can I have this in my real life? The non-magical lakehouse life? The 'I have three kids in sports and work full-time' life?" So, I shared what I do and then did what I always do: I empowered *her* to do the work. *Her* work.

For me, typically, Sundays are my days when my phone won't go on until later in the afternoon, when I am getting ready to plan my week and write out my calendar. This allows me time with family and being fully present, instead of thinking of social content or my week ahead. It gives hubby and me time to review our weeks and discuss where we can help each other.

I also have timers set to tell me when to put my phone away; for example, when I pick up kids from school, my goal is always to be emotionally available for that first hour, when they have lots to say and the excitement of the day is high. During that time, my phone is typically on airplane mode or in my kSafe.

A kSafe is a plastic box with a lock on the lid and a timer. Once I set the timer, I cannot get my phone until the timer goes off. This has allowed me to focus and be present with my people.

My phone also sleeps in a different room from me; she isn't allowed in my bedroom. These tiny changes have made it possible for my brain to be on airplane mode, undistracted and focused on what's in front of me or who is in front of me, and it has allowed me the freedom to feel the joy of being where my feet are.

I didn't make all these changes at once. My rule of thumb is one thing at a time, and if I cannot do it for thirty days without falling back into an old pattern, I start again. I go back to day one.

?

Your phone is not the only reason you struggle with autopilot, but with this work, I have seen it be one of the biggest reasons for getting back on the beam and being present, being where your feet are, and truly making the unconscious conscious.

#teamairplanemode

As you move into the work of this chapter and committing to regular airplane mode time, I want you to do it from a place of questioning everything with excitement.

Imagine if I could just enjoy my Sunday with my people and what's in front of me and not be distracted by my Monday and what awaits me. Is that possible? The answer is yes. With dedication to this practice, it is.

When my lassies on retreat hand me their phones for three days, it is so challenging. Yet all of them claim their anxiety is gone during that time and feel more present and connected.

If being present has been a challenge in the past, this chapter and this work is for you.

THE WORK

Follow Airplane Mode

o The idea of turning my phone on airplane mode for an afternoon makes me feel:

o What exciting benefits could I have by putting my phone on airplane mode?

o List the joys you know you would experience if you had some periods of airplane mode in your life?

o List your excuses for why you would not be ok turning your phone off one afternoon a week:

o No excuses! I am committed to joining #teamairplanemode and will start this week on _____ for _____ number of hours.

As a coach, here are some things I have heard:

- "My phone being in another room won't work for me. I am a deep sleeper."

Try one of those alarms for rooms. They are so fancy now, and they even wake you up with morning meditations. You are welcome!

- "I am a single mum. I cannot put my phone on airplane mode."

One single-mum friend told me she got a landline for her ex-husband for when he has their children, just in case. So, no excuses, lassies! Where there is a will, there is a way.

- "I work from my phone. My clients just wouldn't put up with my phone being off."

We teach people how to treat us, lassies and lads. Let that sink in for a second. If you make yourself available 24/7, then that's what will be expected.

I would say start small here: "I will be out of pocket Sunday until 3:00 p.m." or "7:00 p.m. onward is family time. I will not have my phone on but will respond first thing in the morning."

> *It is amazing how much easier it gets, when you start to see how good it feels.*

CHAPTER 6

UnFollow Bullying our Bodies

"To be beautiful means to be yourself. You don't need to be accepted by others. You need to accept yourself."
—Thich Nhat Hanh

"**W**ell, someone looks like they had a good time in America," he said and chuckled. He snickered and looked at my other relative, who agreed, and they both laughed. He is a family member.

I was a typical young female: unsure of myself, yet attempting to appear confident. I was twenty.

America was where my obsession with food and size and my weight began. Growing up, I was a skinny Scottish lassie. In fact, it bothered me deeply when people called me that. I grew up as a long-distance runner.

On race day, I didn't talk to anyone, because I was so extremely focused on winning, I didn't want anyone in my head.

At the start line, I would overhear, "What's your PB?" (personal best). I was only focused on me, and getting across the line first.

I had the best trainer: my dad. I was the firstborn, and he was told I was going to the Olympics, so we trained six days a week. I had skills and strategy. I would stay behind the winner, letting her shield me from the Scottish winter winds, and at the last 200 meters or so, I would come out from behind her and sprint. I never, ever looked back. I never looked to see

?   61

where she was, but I would hear, "Watch her, the wee one. Watch her, she is right behind you, the wee one."

My whole life, I heard I was "the wee one."

"The wee one to watch," is what the newspapers would say.

Since our most practiced thoughts or the thoughts we hear others say about us become our belief about ourselves, I was, in my mind, *the wee one*.

I replied to that family member "Ohhh, yeah, the food is good in America." My insides felt like someone had punched me over and over. I still remember where I was, who said the words, and every ounce of shame that came with it.

The comments continued about my weight gain, and the shame deepened. *Ugh*. I can feel that shame now, as I share this with you. One thing that is important to me as writer is that you, the reader, know I am on this journey of healing and I am doing it with you. I am not healed. I am not done. I never will be. I will, layer by layer, grow alongside you. Sometimes, my lessons will come first, and I will share them. Other times, yours will.

I am not healed from binging. I am not healed from days of hating myself and my body. I am aware, I am knowing, I am growing, and I am sharing.

"Shame cannot live in the light, lassies."

"Mum, I am going to try Weight Watchers. I have to lose this ten pounds."

Parts of this book are more painful than others to write. Why? My body was simply transitioning from a young athlete to a woman with hips and curves. And rather than having that normalized, I tried to fight the change because of comments from others. But in that moment, that exact moment of attending my first Weight Watchers meeting at age twenty, that was the beginning of what would become almost two decades of fighting my body and what it meant for us: the size it desired, the hips it wished to grow, and the thicker thighs it sought.

I thought that these changes were taking me away from being "the wee one." She was the only body and person I had ever identified with. This transition felt too hard, too much, too painful.

At 105 pounds, I wasn't allowed to talk about my new 115-pound body, right? The wee one didn't tell anyone she felt fat. How could she? She would be greeted with, "Don't be silly. There isn't a pick on you." Or, "You're daft. Don't be daft—you having a laugh?"

So, she did what the wee ones do. She keeps her mouth shut. She followed the knowing that she was not permitted to speak her true feelings. So, she shamefully felt unworthy—gross and shamed by her new body appearance. She secretly attended her Weight Watchers meeting with her mum, who had been by her side, supporting her, since the day she was born. She diligently counted points, and therein began years of yo-yo dieting.

On Weight Watchers, I lost the weight. Then, ate, gained weight, and back to meetings I went. Eventually, the high and impact of the first diet weight-loss never returned, and I sought other ways to reach it. I tried new diet after new diet after new fad; I tried Whole30, no carbs, no sugar, and Keto.

Another night came and another round of shameful feelings for falling off the food wagon. I opened the drawer beside my sink. There they were: those magic pills. Not the diet pills. Those had worked but I'd quit them a long time ago. The *other* pills. The ones that come in a green box; the ones you can buy in packs of thirty-six and cost around ten dollars. The ones you can locate in any grocery store; the ones you can hide amongst your groceries. The ones I never ran out of and had in every handbag, makeup bag, and in the bathroom cabinet. The ones that took away my shame. The *laxatives*.

The box says take one or two. In the end, I was taking six to eight every evening. The evening meant around 2:00 or

3:00 a.m., when everyone was asleep. I would wake up in a panic, the pains in my stomach so horrific, they mirrored contractions. Yet, night after night, the same pattern continued. I sat on the toilet for forty-five minutes while my entire bowel emptied. Sometimes, I passed out from the pain. I vowed never to take them again, but the next night, I opted to cut back instead of just cut it all out. I told no one, of course. No one.

One night, I found myself crying while reading online. I couldn't do one more diet, and I couldn't hate myself anymore. To my surprise, I read that taking laxatives is a sign of disordered eating. I consider myself an intelligent lassie. Yet, we cannot see that which we seek not to see.

I loved waking up to a flat stomach. For a decade, I destroyed myself and destroyed my insides for a flat stomach; for a feeling that took away my shame of binging, emotional eating, overeating, and not sticking to whatever fad diet I was taking on.

> *"People often say that beauty is in the eye of the beholder,*
> *and I say that the most liberating thing about beauty*
> *is realizing you are the beholder."*
> —Salma Hayek

Turns out, my struggle is a struggle of many women. Perhaps you didn't use laxatives or diet pills. Perhaps you didn't binge or subscribe to the diet culture. And yet, the shame associated with weight, food consumption, and body image takes up more thought space than it should.

But who am I without it? Who are you? What are we? If we aren't consumed by thoughts about food, of our body shape and size, or of the next diet, then what? Diet culture is a billion-dollar industry. How do we unlearn this? How do we go against the societal norms that skinny is the only beauty? How then do we truly *UnFollow*?

"I can't," she sobbed. "I can't..."

The mirror stared at her, and she stared at the mirror. Seven other women sat on the sofa, scared to breathe, pained, knowing they would be next.

I stood beside her. I placed my hands on her chest and on her back, and I encouraged her to breathe.

She said quietly, "I like my elbows." She sobbed more. We all quietly sobbed with her. We collectively hugged her.

Healing collectively is where one woman struggles to think of anything she loves about herself, and other trusting, soulful lassies come forward and do it for her, with her.

We have not only healed. We have lived. Truly lived.

If you are collectively healing and not collectively living, you are missing out on this ONE.Life.

We transitioned to pairs. We faced our partner, we held hands, we gazed into each other's eyes, and we took turns saying the things we love about each other.

We were closing the end of our three-day retreat at The Magical Lakehouse. We had scaled waterfalls together. We had completed level-4 whitewater rafting, where we all thought we might die (we are a dramatic bunch). We'd picked apples and made homemade pie together. We'd written letters and burned them. We had laughed and cried.

"I love how you went first under the waterfall. That was so brave."

"I love how you talk about your co-parenting. It's so beautiful."

"Your smile makes me smile."

"You shared first, and it helped me feel brave enough to share."

"You are so smart. I could listen to you talk all day."

Minutes passed. Tears flowed down the lassies' faces as they heard things they had never heard before, things they wondered about themself. Hearing it brought both peace and pain in one swift blow. The room was transforming—these

?

lassies were transforming. They were beginning to believe. Beginning to know.

Do you know what lassies and butterflies have in common?

Butterflies cannot see their wings, so they literally have no idea how beautiful they are. They fly around while people literally stop mid-sentence to comment on their sheer beauty. How many times have you heard someone say, "Look at that butterfly!"?

How often have you thought to yourself how beautiful your friend is, how brave your sister is, how smart your husband is, how resilient your kid is? Like the butterfly, we lassies fail to see our own beauty inside and out. We fail to feel our own beauty.

Imagine a world where we don't have to be on a retreat to hear these words? Imagine if we tell our sister in a random call how brave she is. Imagine if you told the Publix grocery clerk that their smile literally makes your day every week.

Imagine if you began to believe the kind words. Imagine if you began to live them and show up as them. And one day, you didn't need to hear them, because *you* knew them. Deep inside your core, you knew them, and they began to be who you knew you were all along.

If it is true that the most important relationship that we have is the one we have with ourselves, and that we can only love others to the extent we love ourselves, then we lassies have work to do.

What if this, lassies, is the most important work we ever do? Choosing to UnFollow Bullying our Bodies due to some of the things you may have heard, or even said…

- The message, "Don't leave the table until your food is finished."

- The subconscious counting points, as we decide what to order at a restaurant, that haunts us, despite there being a decade of no Weight Watchers meetings.

- As we walk the grocery aisle, our hand just goes for the laxatives without even thinking.

- We catch ourselves thinking someone "shouldn't wear that," because, in our mind, they are overweight.

- We promise no more diets yet find ourselves falling victim to the next fad.

- We catch a glimpse of a post about the latest new drug to help weight loss.

- We find ourselves standing on a scale, despite our promise to not allow a scale to tell us if we are worthy or not.

Hearing something and living something are two very different things. This work may be the most important work for the females of our generation. When we love ourselves, we judge ourselves less. And when we judge ourselves less, we judge others less. Imagine. Imagine that world.

How can we collectively heal this? How can we heal our nutritional trauma and say *no* to diet culture and be the example our children and peers need?

What if we stopped allowing our brains to bully our bodies? What if this was the year to *UnFollow* diet culture? What if your inner rebel said, "I love my body"?

Loving your body doesn't mean you like every part of it. Hello! I have an arse that looks like the moon, and I have stretch marks that look like I was fighting with a real-life Mummabear and did not win. There will probably never be a day I view those as attractive or beautiful. But that doesn't mean I don't love her.

My body birthed twins—two babies at the same freaking time. She carried them full-term; she made four lungs, two hearts, four eyes, four arms, and four legs, at the same freaking time. Talk about badass. She also breastfed them for eleven months, at the same time her first born fought stage 4 cancer. How could you hate someone who did that for you? *What?*

How could you allow a brain to bully her? How could you think laxatives would make you love her more? They never did.

It's been years of unraveling my obsession with dieting and yo-yo diets and abuse of my body. My biggest regret is keeping it a secret. What happened when I started coaching lassies was that I discovered almost every lassie has some issue with their body. It was then I decided I needed to add this work to the intimacy of my retreats, where women felt safe to look into a full-length mirror, sometimes for the first time in their life.

With the help of an intuitive eating expert, I was able to begin to heal myself at the same time as the women I worked with. It began with a full-length mirror, watching other women bare their souls, cry, and be truthful. It began by holding hands and eye-gazing with a brave lassie who told me things I didn't see.

A fire roared, and a storm brewed outside by the lake, and yet inside, there was calmness, a heart nod. A heart nod to every woman in the room—we got this. A heart nod that said, together, we can heal this. Alone is not the answer. It continues with the writing of this chapter, sharing things I never have, in the hope someone feels a sense of hope and knowing they are not alone.

So, I heart-nod you, lassie. You are so beautiful. Your smile. Your eyes. Your soul. Showing your flaws only makes you more so. Together, let's vow to stop this anguish of self-destruction.

THE WORK

Follow Learning to Love our Bodies

"Your body hears everything your mind says."
—Naomi Judd

What if we stopped allowing our brains to bully our bodies? "I love my body" doesn't mean I have to like everything about it. But it *does* mean I stop my brain from bullying her.

Enter this work thinking of your future self, your favorite version of yourself, the one who doesn't bully her body every day. The one who speaks kindly to her body and doesn't judge her or others. When you get excited about that version, only then begin asking all the questions.

Questioning everything with excitement is a method for living. It's where we choose to not only heal, but live. It's where we decide to not only think but *do*!

Your body loves you. She has proven this time and time again. Now, show her some love by healing some open wounds you still have.

This work helps you to *UnFollow* society defining what our body should look like and making the decision *you* will define it! Year after year, we criticize our bodies, and it hasn't changed anything; so, it's time to change the status quo and, instead, do the work and Follow learning to love our bodies.

This is your reminder that you do not need to love every part of your body in order to be kind to it. What if you begin this work by treating your body the way you hope your daughter treats hers, the way you pray your son treats his? Sometimes, the thought of loving our bodies is too far-fetched; but imagining it's your daughter's, your mother's, your best friend's, that changes your mindset and leads you on the path of healing.

- o List all the things your body has done for you. Don't stop until you get to at least twenty.
- o Write a letter to your body, apologizing for the way you have bullied it, including the things you have made her miss out on. Then, burn it!
- o UnFollowing all the abuse you did to her requires you to replace it with a new following. Write a letter on how you plan to treat her, going forward. How you plan to learn to love her. Write it from a place of joy and excitement and possibility. No shame can live in this letter! Laminate it! Put it on your mirror. Have it in plain sight, read it every day, until your mind no longer bullies your body.
- o Write on a Post-it: "I love my body and everything she has done for me." Place it somewhere you see it daily.

CHAPTER 7

UnFollow Diet Culture

"The diet industry is the only business in the world that succeeds by failing you."

—Unknown

"**H**i, honey."
"Hi."

"Guess what? I am on Keto again. I've lost seventeen pounds in two weeks."

A diet is defined as a special course of food to which one restricts oneself, either to lose weight or for medical reasons.

Restrict being the important word here.

Diets don't work.

None of them.

Let me restate that: Diets don't work in a sustainable healthy way.

They work in the short term. Case in point, the seventeen pounds she lost in two weeks.

Why don't diets work? Well, our bodies are so bloody smart, aren't they? They are designed to keep us alive. I know, right? So, when we have our cheat day or fall off the so-called diet wagon or have a treat, we turn into ravenous pigs who cannot stop eating. Why? It's not because we lack discipline. It's not because we don't know better. It's because our bodies are geniuses! Literally. They are keeping us alive and think, "Guys, we don't know when we will eat again, so let's up the ghrelin hormone. That will increase her hunger and get us the food we need."

No, really. *That's* what happens. I know. I'm upset, too. Irritated, to say the least. But lassies, when we know better, we do better, right?

At the same time as the ghrelin, our hunger hormone, increases, our leptin hormone decreases, which is our "feeling full" hormone. So, basically, we are screwed. I believe that is the technical term. Is this a good time to mention that calorie restriction actually slows down your metabolism? After years of yo-yo dieting, I totally messed up my metabolism. Since I am little Miss Me-responsible, I started looking at ways to fix that. That is when I found the intuitive eating experts, Dr. Will Cole's work and former nurse, Victoria Yates.

I will be honest, the idea of intuitive eating terrified me. *Me?* Trust *Me?* With food? Not sure that's a great idea. My all-or-nothing mindset with food has cost me so much energy and time, the idea that, somehow, I could move away from it and trust my body to signal me about hunger cues? Is that a joke? Never have I ever eaten one slice of anything. And, hello, did you read Chapter Two?

For some reason, I became fascinated.

I started to think about what my future self would do. What would my favorite version of me do? As I approached forty, I started to wonder—would I eat this way forever? Will I just yo-yo diet and go up and down in weight forever? Will I isolate myself from events when I am on a diet and consume everything in the buffet when I am not? Will I overthink a date night because I am on a diet and eat three courses and some of his food when I am not? How does someone who is an all-in personality type trust themself to eat intuitively?

When you ask questions with excitement, everything changes. What if I somehow was comfortable enough at a party that I didn't consume every appetizer offered to me? What if I was able to mindfully eat and not consume food like I'm fifteen years old again at the dinner table, where the fastest eater was the winner because food was served family style? What if I knew when I was full and stopped? What if I knew I was full? Just full?

What if I didn't count calories in my head as I made my plate? What if I could eat intuitively and pursue health goals at the same time? What if the misconceptions about intuitive eating have been keeping me from *food Freedom?* What would I do with this brain space, if it wasn't focused on food?

What if, like you, we didn't fail diets—all ninety-five percent of us who go on them? What if our bodies are just geniuses, trying to keep us alive, and most of our work is mindset?

I had so many misconceptions about intuitive eating. I mean, to be fair, some of the information out there makes it look like I get to eat whatever I want and be skinny. I can confirm, lassies, this is false.

I said to Victoria Yates, my favorite nurse and intuitive eating expert in this area, during an interview on my podcast, *Coaching and a Cup of Tea with Mummabear,* "Can I undo this damage and relearn to trust myself? To trust my body?"

She said something that changed my life.

"Melissa, it was not your body saying, 'Please, feed me everything in your fridge, and when you're done, consume the entire pantry.' Nor did your body say, 'Yes, we should eat the entire pizza, even though we don't love pizza.' That is not intuitive eating. That was your brain releasing hormones because of dieting. Your body didn't make the request."

Something shifted inside of me. Maybe, just maybe, I can figure this out.

My body actually craves really good, whole foods. That's how I was raised, on veggies, whole foods, and supplements.

Intuitive eating isn't a new concept. In fact, in 1995, Evelyn Tribole and Elyse Resh wrote a book called *Intuitive Eating.* The concept was developed to heal our relationships with food and our bodies.

❓

OMG! This is exactly what I need. Well, me and the ninety-five percent of us living in the "We Failed Yet Another Diet" camp.

Intuitive eating is a research-based, non-diet approach to listening to our body's signals for when to start eating and for when you're full and should stop. It's a lifelong practice, and it's one myself and my clients take on. We are in it for the long run.

For twenty years, Dan Buettner (*The Blue Zones*) traveled the globe and identified five blue zones—areas that have the highest population of centurions (people over aged 100). His research found, in these five regions, one common thread: they eat until they are eighty-percent full. This is a common target in Intuitive Eating. In the documentary, *Live to 100: Secrets of the Blue Zones,* he found that one of the pillars to living a joyful and healthy life past 100 years old was walking. Not aggressive exercise. *Walking.* Sign me up!

Dr. Will Cole says you can't heal a body you hate, so the idea of good and bad foods doesn't help us love ourselves more. Instead, it leads us to hate and stress, which only harm our body more.

How exciting it is to imagine we heal our relationship with food and that healing allows us to live. *Really live.* We can attend the event. We can go on the date night. Neither activity scares us, thinking it's all or nothing with food. In fact, we are excited to try the new foods. We know when we are hungry and when we are full.

This is living.

❓

THE WORK

Follow Intuitive Eating

"Honor your hunger, honor your fullness, honor yourself."

—Unknown

o When I imagine my relationship with food is healed, I can see:

o I want to trust my body's hunger cues and full cues because:

o I am doing this for:

o List three things that would prevent you from becoming an Intuitive Eater:

As a coach, things I've heard from clients:
- I could never trust myself around all foods. I just don't buy any bad foods, so I don't cave in.

First of all, we don't use the word *never*. Second, what if, instead of isolating yourself from foods and the world, you focused more on how you will feel after healing your relationship with food and can trust yourself around any food?

❓

- I don't know when I am hungry or when I am full.

Lassie— Hello, and same. I said these exact words. Truth is, it requires slowing down. It requires enjoying food in a mindful eating manner, not while you are standing up, watching TV, and packing your kids' lunches. It requires planning, and Intuitive Eating Misconception #1,000,035 is we can't have plans, if we are eating intuitively.

That's false information. I don't know about you, sweet reader, but four kids ages eleven and under, a husband who travels for work, a few pets, and the several companies I run— Yeah, this lassie be planning.

- I want to start, but I'm scared I will gain weight.

Hello! Same, again. Most people lose weight and then it levels off, but if you're chronically underweight, your body will likely put weight on, because, well, it needs it. But the truth is, your body is a genius. It knows where you need to be, and it will stay there, knowing you aren't starving it.

o   If I wasn't scared to put on weight, I would:

I am committing to a new relationship with food. One where I can be at a party and not consume everything at the buffet. One where I know there is chocolate in the freezer and yet I eat just a chunk after dinner.

I am committing to being able to enjoy a meal out without feeling all or nothing. I am attracted to whole foods, as they make me feel so good. I am healing my relationship with food for me, but also for my daughter, my sons, my husband, and to every person I have the honor of coaching. I know I don't need to do this perfectly, but I know I need to do it.

o   Now, write your intention around healing your relationship with food:

o   Write it on a Post-it note, and place it where you can see it daily.

CHAPTER 8

UnFollow Fix all the Trauma

"Trauma is not what happens to you. Trauma is what happens inside you, as a result of what happens to you."
—Dr. Gabor Maté

"Nope, you are not leaving the table until you have finished your dinner," I say.

This wave of emotion comes over me. That feeling of "I've lived this moment before." Nothing is coming up.

Wait. The emotion comes over me again. It can't be.

Dear God, I have. I *have*. *I have*. It hits me like a double-decker bus. This is what I heard growing up! But now I am living 4,000 miles away from the table where I heard these words, and I'm saying the exact same words to my own children. How can this be?

It is not lost on me that we are the first generation to be healing ourselves at the same time we are raising families. Never before in time has this happened.

A wise lassie once told me, "You know, Melissa, you're going to mess your kids up. Your job is to mess them up the least amount possible..."

Before you get all excited at my agreeing to this and setting the bar extremely low for us parents, hear me out. Have you ever met an adult with zero issues? Zero childhood or otherwise-type issues? *Exactly*! And really, do not feel sorry for my bairns. They live a deeply enchanted childhood—just ask them.

Yesterday, they said, and I quote, "Having a Scottish mum is the worst! *Ohhh*, 'sleep good, feel good.' We are changing it to, 'Sleep bad, feel good.'"

My other loving son decides it's his opportunity to contribute to the conversation,

"Oh, how about, 'Oh, let me check the ingredients. Nope, sorry guys, twenty-three grams of sugar. This isn't for us.'"

"Yeah, Mum just reads too much."

"Why can't she just be cool like (they name a mum whom I refuse to name here; call me petty, I don't care). She doesn't set bedtimes. You can eat what you want and do what you want."

I'm the worst. Imagine me as a mum, checking ingredients and setting bedtimes—someone call child services!

Kid: "Mum, why can't you just be cool in front of our friends?"

Me: "I am *not* cool guys. In order for me to be cool with your friends, I would need to be cool with mine. Therein lies the root of the problem." Case in point. #iamnotcool

So, I have resigned myself to knowing that my kids will have issues and I should save money for therapy. Perhaps it will be my unresolved food trauma that I am working through. Nothing motivates me more to getting it together than this. But at the same time, how boring would adult life be if you were perfect? No?

"Mum, look! I'm sixty-two pounds."

The kids start piling onto the Publix, a local grocery store, lobby scale.

"Move! I was on it first!"

"No, you move. I was!"

"Dude, move!"

I said, "Okay, guys. Come on."

"Well, I'm sixty-four pounds so..."

I replied, "Wow, you are getting so strong."

I have had very complicated relationships with scales my whole life. Daily weighing. Then never weighing. To weekly weighing. To throwing the scales out. To buying new, fancy body-fat scales. This... This is breaking generational trauma. This moment, right here. Often, we expect *big* massive shifts, big moments, huge epiphanies; but what we get is a moment where your kids find it fun to weigh themselves and believe that the higher the weight, the stronger you are.

I didn't have that growing up. A pound heavier meant fatter to me. Meant worse to me. Meant wrong. Meant bad. So, while my kids or your kids may not have the perfect relationship with every element of their weight or their body image, imagine if they just didn't have scalexiety?

Scalexiety is a term I use to describe the horror and pain of standing on a scale. The pain of that number meaning I am good or bad, fat or thin, worthy or unworthy. The deep dread. No matter how I feel before I stand on that scale, the feeling would change completely in a matter of seconds. The waiting of the red line to turn to a number and *poof*! Just like that, I'm sent into a downward spiral of all-or-nothing binging, and my inner rebel of "whatever, it doesn't matter what I do—nothing works." Or, "Yes, girl. You did it! You lost a few pounds. You go. You look amazing. Wow—nice job, lassie." All of this determined by a machine that knows nothing about me, doesn't care about me, and is operated by a freaking battery.

Lassies and lads, look for what I call the mini-magical moments. The small yet significant moments when you can breathe, knowing the work you are doing is changing generations to come, beginning with your people. Hundreds of mini-magical moments lead to you living the favorite version of your ONE.Life.

We place too much pressure on ourselves to be perfect to pass down none of the parts of us we don't like. And yet, if we are truly living, this will happen sometimes, even subconsciously. For those things we are consciously aware of, it is time to break those—but only from a place of joy and want and excitement, not from shame or blame or lack of responsibility.

> *Look for what I call the mini-magical moments. The small yet significant moments when you can breathe, knowing the work you are doing is changing generations to come, beginning with your people.*

I cannot even count the number of clients who deal with this.

They enter the world of healing and exit the world of living.

Do not enter the world of healing and exit the world of living.

They want to heal every trauma and trigger and the faster the better, as then their kids or partner are less likely to be impacted. In theory, yes. In living, no.

In fact, when we take on too much healing or do it too quickly, we tend to stop living, to become deeply overwhelmed and stressed, and, in fact, we are triggered even more.

When we choose to live, when we choose to do this work with excitement and joy, knowing it's working, everything changes. But it can only happen one mini-magical moment at a time, as we build this ONE.Life. Nothing more, nothing less.

This is why my clients tell me their wins every session. This is why I create a wall of wins when I travel with my kids. It helps us notice those mini-magical moments that build the ONE.Life we seek.

❓

THE WORK

Follow Break Generational Trauma, One Trauma at a Time

"Healing is a daily event. You can't 'go somewhere' to be healed: you must go inward to be healed. This means a daily commitment to doing the work."
—Dr. Nicole LePera, The Holistic Psychologist

Our purpose is not to create a perfect life for our kids or our people. It is to show our humanness and to raise our kids to know they are deeply loved by their deeply imperfect parents. And to show our people we are flawed humans who are doing the best with what we know, right now.

Our work is to become aware of our traumas and triggers and the impacts they can have, if unchecked, and then to decide which ones have the biggest impact on our people.

Have you ever met an adult with no issues? No parent issues or people-pleasing, boundary issues or control issues? Me, neither... Not sure I want to or need to, either.

What if, each year, we focused on different parts of ourselves instead of tackling all our trauma and hoping we can be perfect for those close to us?

It can be so overwhelming, when you begin work in your life with a coach, mentor, therapist, guide, or pastor. Instead, pick one thing, and focus on that! Shift that! Grow in that area!

o   This year, my big focus will be:

o   While I am doing this for me, I know

_____ will also be hugely impacted.

o   The reason I choose this for my yearly goal is:

o   When I feel like I am not making real progress, I will
    pay attention to mini-magical moments by:

o   Actions I will take include:

o   My triggers around this trauma are:

o   I want to show up for my people in the following way:
    By showing my people my human, imperfect side, I
    am giving them a gift of:

Focusing on one per year will shift the all-or-nothing
thinking. It will calm the inner rebel and also
UnFollow that "in order to be great humans, we must
be healed" false narrative.

More of us talking about what we are healing, and why, is
how we collectively change and encourage others. Through
bravery and belief, not shame and perfectionism.

It is only by living we truly heal!

So, let's live, lassies and lads, and show our imperfect
selves as we do it.

> ***It is only by living we truly
> heal!***

CHAPTER 9

UnFollow Martyrdom Mountain

*"What if the call of motherhood is not to be a martyr
but to be a model?*

—Glennon Doyle

The one with the most kids wins. The one who loses themself most wins. The one who suffers the most wins. The one with the kid who has the most disorders, wins. The one who is single wins. The one who is on every school committee wins. The one whose spouse cheats wins. The one whose... Fill in the blank.

If you wanted to skip this chapter, because it triggered you—good. It triggered me to write it. Can we have a hug before you read it? Yes, of course. Hold a little longer, longer... Don't let go yet, please. I am scared. You are, too. But we can do hard things, and we will. So, we will face this together. I can even go first.

"Hi, I am Melissa. I am a mum who has martyred herself in the name of her children. I have, on many occasions, chosen to die rather than live in the name of my kids. My son had cancer, my other children have dyslexia, anxiety, and ADHD. My daughter had craniosynostosis, and she was adopted. I am a recovering alcoholic with no family in this country! I have a husband who is a trial attorney and travels."

Should I stop?

If the triggering is happening again, just know, this chapter gets better. This chapter will hold your hand and walk you down from Martyrdom Mountain to an EMPOWERED.Life. So, don't leave before the magic happens.

Did you know flamingos lose their pinkness as they birth their baby flamingos? Their *flaminglets* (isn't that so cute?). I am currently staying at The Hidden Flamingo, hence the reference, a beautiful Airbnb owned by Jill.

Jill reached out to me, to join my EMPOWERED.Life six-month intensive coaching program.

"I am terrified. I have never invested in myself," she said.

"Let's meet for a cup of tea," I told her. Jill appeared to know a lot about me, but I wanted to get to know her, and there is nothing quite like an in-person meeting.

Jill drives a fun Jeep. When she picked me up, the roof was off, and we blared music and laughed. Jill is fun, but she seemed worn out. Jill is what social media psychologists have coined "a giver."

She went over a wide range of job-like activities and things she did for others, and I was confused, because she was not being paid for most of them, and yet she was an entrepreneur. Jill had taken on the role of being the primary earner in her family of three, and it suited her, as she is a go-getter.

Jill isn't an overly emotional person. You wouldn't imagine she is a crier, and yet tears filled her eyes. She removed her glasses and wiped her eyes. "I am sorry, I don't know what's wrong with me... I don't cry."

"First—never apologize for crying. Crying is the love-language of our soul. It is permission to let go. You are letting go. You are also saying things you never say but think over and over, am I right?" And also, I make everyone cry eventually.

Jill nodded...

Jaxon, Jill's only child, has required Jill's full attention since he was little, due to a diagnosis of autism. When I met Jill, she had never been away from Jaxon more than a few hours. Jaxon was ten at the time and being homeschooled, after countless failed attempts to get him what he needed via the public-school system. I have watched Jaxon have what I would describe as an episode, and Jill handled it with grace and respect for her and for him. This life, all of it, was burning her out. She needed a change and a shift inside her and her family unit.

Yet, when I met Jill, she wasn't ready to let go of the reins. She claimed no one else could do what she does, and this was her life. Jill and I had tea from Martyrdom Mountain. I know it well, as I have lived there. A sick kiddo or a child with special needs leads many of us up the mountain, and yet, when we start to *UnFollow* that path and take a new course, our lives can change completely.

You see, on Martyrdom Mountain, there are no solutions.

In fact, any solutions presented to you while on the mountain will be shot down, because, well, we are comfortable there. People say, "How do you do it?" and "You are such a selfless mum," if not to our face, behind our backs. We are commended for our selflessness.

You will rarely hear me talk of my son's cancer diagnosis without mentioning I was thirty-eight weeks pregnant with twins. I may or may not *Follow* it up with some story about how I breastfed them for eleven months, while my son was in New York or Philly for his treatments, and when I couldn't be with my baby boy twins, I would freeze the milk and FedEx it to them. Imagine the accolades, lassies.

Here is the issue, lassies: I almost killed myself, trying to support my twenty-month-old son with his stage 4 cancer diagnosis, and breast pumping or feeding the twins every few hours was brutal on my body.

Cannon had just been through a thirteen-hour surgery. He was on life support for five days. I never left his side, not once. And my mum and sister would bring my sons, Arran and Gray, who were just a few months old, to the hospital. I would breastfeed them, and they would leave. I am all for "breast is best," if you can, but at what cost? Had I walked down from the mountain, lassies, perhaps I would have seen that living on coffee, soda, and hospital food, barely eating, while sleeping very little and breastfeeding two boys was not sustainable and frankly downright dangerous. I could have seen that this was making me sick. That I needed to let that go and instead focus on Cannon and being physically and mentally strong for him.

But when you live on that mountain long enough, there is little that can be done until you face burnout. No one pulled me aside and said, "Melissa, put your kids on formula. Rest. Be ready for Cannon when he wakes up." And I did not have the tools to question myself.

Jill didn't have the tools, either—yet.

No one questioned Jill, because, guess what? Everyone around her was winning, so why would they? They had an invested self-interest in her being on the mountain. Why would they dare call her down? What incentive did they have? Her family, people she worked for, for free, were all winning. Jill was not.

Yet, here Jill was, wiping tears from her eyes and apologizing to me, someone she had never met in person. This was my sign: she was ready. She was ready for my hard questions, she was ready for the changes, and she was ready to do the work and win at her ONE.Life.

I started asking Jill some hard but exciting questions. I had her rate the main areas of her life on a scale of one to ten, to help us decide in which area we would start. I asked questions like, "Jill, how do you define success? Are you happy? What do you want out of this ONE.Life?"

After twelve months of getting excited about her life and asking the right questions, Jill got back her pink, which she had lost. She was no longer the pink flamingo who lost her pink in the name of her child in her ONE.Life. She was no longer having tea on Martyrdom Mountain.

Jill got her pink back, like the Mumma flamingo, and she gained it back bit by bit. Choice by choice. Action by action. Exciting question after exciting question. She started to get excited about what was possible, because the questions came from a place of what is next. What would your favorite version of yourself do? How could this be exciting?

It got very exciting for Jill and her family.

Jill sold everything, including her home in the city. She moved her husband and son to the beach. She bought bikes, kayaks, paddleboards, and surfboards, and she now runs a successful adventure company, Beyond the Waves, in gorgeous New Smyrna Beach, Florida. She and her sister bought condos there, and she rents them out. She has her son and husband working every day in the new family adventure company.

One question that I asked her very matter-of-factly, but which Jill says stood out and changed everything, was, "So tell me, who are you, when you are not Jaxon's mum?" She didn't know. After several hours of digging into this, it became very clear to me that, when we set goals for Jill, we also needed to set goals for Jaxon. Jill wanted Jaxon to have relationships outside of her; she deeply desired independence for him. But for Jill to be okay, Jaxon needed to be okay. We had to start there.

After years of setting goals with hundreds of people, I developed The VOTE Method, a strategy that allows my clients and me to set goals. But, better than that, it actually allows them to achieve the goals.

Many lassies and lads don't achieve their goals—or, as I like to say, don't VOTE on themselves, because they don't know how. Let's be honest everyone has their own way of setting and achieving goals, and if you have a system that works for you, stick to it. Truth be told, who has time to read fifteen books on goal-setting or attend three-day conferences to figure out how to set them?

I set out to develop something that saved my clients time and energy and was extremely effective. This method takes you through eight questions that essentially help you VOTE on whether you really want the goal or not. It really works, and you can have access to the workshop on The VOTE Method at melissawiggins.life.

So, we set goals for Jill and Jaxon, and everything has changed for their family. Jaxon has a beautiful, soulful relationship with his dad. He has a personal trainer he works out with, without Jill being present. Jaxon can be without Jill for full days while she works on promoting Beyond the Waves on the beach or while taking people on kayak tours to see dolphins and manatees. I have had the honor of spending time and coaching this entire family, and, well, they make a Scottish lassie cry, because they did the work and the work changed everything for their ONE.Life.

Jill's worries about what her son would do as he got older are no more. She built a company that, someday, will be his. She left the city life and every obligation that went with it. She stopped being the host of every single celebration, which, in America is, well, a lot. She hired a personal trainer and got healthy with her family. She walks with me weekly in my walking group, even though it's an hour drive from the beach to attend. She even started a beach version of Women Who Walk Win!

It may have taken several years for her to get there, but once she started answering the hard questions like, "Why have you been doing the bookkeeping for your friend, for free?" and "What if Jaxon doesn't have a regular job?" "Why do you host every holiday?" and "Why do you think you are so tired?". She became more aware of what she wanted to focus on for her and her family's future.

It was then, and only then, that we shifted to the exciting questions like, "What kind of job could you imagine Jaxon doing?" "What job would make you feel energized to get out of bed in the morning?" "How could your life look, living at the beach?" "How would you feel working for yourself?" "How would it feel to make yourself a priority?" And "What will you do with all this freedom?"

This is when everything changed.

?

Question everything with excitement, lassies and lads. *Everything.* Choosing to *UnFollow* is a way of life. It's a choice followed by action.

The reason this work is best done with a mentor, coach, therapist, or confidant is because it requires asking questions, and, frankly, our brains are not wired for that. Our brains like comfort and autopilot. Yet, add a coach, and every question is just that—a question, a curiosity, a glimpse into the future of what could be.

I told Jill, like I tell all my clients, this work is really data collecting. The answers to the questions are not graded, judged, or shamed. They are, however, data. They are information for us to collect and/or use to help with making decisions. Making no decision, asking no questions—well, that is a decision, and it's one that keeps you stuck.

We have created an unspoken contract as mums. It's called the Suffering Olympics. Those who suffer and lose themselves the most, they get the trophy. They get the passes, they get accolades—the Selfless Awards.

I want a new contract. I want the contract that has a clause (can you tell I'm a lawyer?) that says, "We mummabears can be happy, joyful, energized, and also have goals and dreams, ones that our kids watch us achieve." Or, in Jill's case, are a part of.

One that we can be mummabears who don't die in our children's name, but instead who live in them. We choose to live.

You can be A Mum And....

I want a contract where we come down from Martyrdom Mountain. We simply *UnFollow* it, and we *Follow* a path to an EMPOWERED.Life. One like Jill not only chose to have but worked to make.

THE WORK

Follow the Path to an EMPOWERED.Life

UnFollow the path to Martyrdom Mountain and head back down to an island I like to call an EMPOWERED.Life.

- o A Mum And... means: who are you when you are not being a Mum. Who are you?
- o What decision have you made, knowing accolades will come from others?
- o How do you define success?
- o On a scale of 1-10 how happy are you?
- o What is one thing you could do that would grade you higher on the happy scale?
- o List all the challenging things that have happened to you in your ONE.Life and how they are keeping you on up on Martyrdom Mountain.
- o Pick one thing that you will work on this year to help you walk back down the mountain to an EMPOWERED.Life.
- o List questions that get you excited about your life.

CHAPTER 10

UnFollow Parent Pleasing

"The only real valuable thing is intuition."
"Intuition does not come to an unprepared mind."
—Albert Einstein

We were on retreat at The Magical Lakehouse, my magical, very remote home in the woods, on a lake, nestled in the foothills of the Blue Ridge Mountains.

"Hey, could we go for a walk?" Diana asked me.

Diana had never been on a retreat before, never had a coach before, and she was excited to get started.

This three-day intensive retreat is a complete reset for the mind, body, and soul. On day one, the lassies sign a contract with me, promising to keep their head where their feet are, and they hand me their phones. My number is given to all the significant others at home, in case of emergency. *Waterfalls and Wonder - The Retreat* is basically summer camp for adults, except we eat completely clean, whole foods and do an entire internal and external reset. So, maybe not quite the same, but it is filled with challenges that change your ONE.Life.

Diana lives in New Jersey, where her parents and siblings live, too.

"I would love to live in Florida... someday," she said softly.

Diana is smart. Like *really* smart. She recently started her own online company, DG Consulting, a bookkeeping service, and made six figures in year one. She is an online bookkeeper helping female entrepreneurs and is so passionate about women making money.

"Someday?" My ears always perk up when people use this word. Mostly because I get curious about what the belief block is that prevents this notion from being a present goal, instead of a far-off, in the distance dream.

"Why someday?"

"Well, my family all live in New Jersey, but New Jersey doesn't feel like home to me. The weather and gray skies and winters are so hard on my mental health."

While family was mentioned in her reasoning, as well as the weather, I knew there was more.

As Diana and I walked in the beautiful woods, we decided to sit. As we sat, we looked down on the lake. Everything was so quiet. The only sounds were the birds chirping and the rustling of the leaves as chipmunks chased one another. The sun was bright and warm, and we sat quietly.

Silence may be our most undervalued tool. So often, we feel wisdom lies in words; yet I have found, for my clients, oftentimes so much more wisdom comes in the silence, just sitting with me. Diana wasn't used to silence. She is driven, hard-working, and works sun up to sun down. A former dancer, she never stops.

But there, nestled in the woods and settled in silence, she had nothing to distract her. No phone, no clients emailing, nowhere to take her twin boys, no husband to check in with. Just her, me, and silence.

Minutes feel like hours in this little bubble I have created at The Magical Lakehouse. Three days feels like three weeks, when you don't have a phone or TV to distract your every thought.

What felt like hours passed before Diana said, "I have always been a good girl. First, I was a dancer who was going professional. I was praised by my parents and their friends, always achieving and pleasing everyone. But I am almost forty, and I am still a good girl. The truth is, I don't think I can move to Florida, because I don't want my parents to be upset with me. But I'm almost forty..."

As a recovering good girl, I can tell you, the belief work around this runs deep, usually for decades.

When I was twenty-six, I moved to the USA. I am the eldest of five kids, and my parents had big dreams of a big wedding. Frankly, I did, too. I had worked in a bridal store when I was in law school, and let's just say I knew the designer of my dress, the price of my dress, and the perfect veil. I wish this was a lie.

I was twenty-six when I first disobeyed my parents. I say *disobeyed* because that's what it felt like. For the first time, they had an opinion on my life that was different than mine, and, for the first time in my life, I wasn't swayed by their disapproval.

"You can't get married at the courthouse," my dad said. My parents got married at twenty, and like all parents, they wanted something different for me. They didn't want the courthouse for me, too.

My family were in Scotland, and Michael and I began planning a wedding in Florida. But then, a few months into the "You can't invite so and so" and "If you invite her, you have to invite him," and, of course, "You can't sit them together," it all became too much for the people-pleaser perfectionist in me.

So, I married at the courthouse, and my parents were crushed. They had the right to feel this way—I was their first born. But the part that's important, lassies and lads, was this was *not* about them. This was about me. I remember telling Michael, "I've never done things my parents didn't want me to. I have never put aside their opinions, but this time, I chose to UnFollow their recommendation and chose to Follow what my future husband and I wanted.

This was the beginning of the process of choosing to UnFollow my parents and Follow myself, embracing my own inner knowing.

That moment there with Diana was exactly that for her, the realization that she had a choice: to live for her parents or to live her own ONE.Life. The life she imagined for her and her kids. Diana loves her parents. I love mine. And yet, we get tangled up in the pleasing of them, often ignoring our own dreams and desires. We do this often with these unwritten contracts, things never spoken, but the actions speak loudly. Or, in Diana's case, the inaction.

The truth is, her "someday" was really, "I don't want to upset my parents and move away. I can't handle the thought of them being upset with me, thinking I'm selfish or not a good daughter." Although she didn't say those words, her actions said them for her.

Tears rolled down my face. It had been one year since I sat in the woods with Diana. Twelve months, fifty-two weeks, 365 days.

"I am here!" she screamed. "I am here. I did it. Matt and I did it. We would not be here without you, and I know, I know, you will tell me that's not true and I did all this work to get here. And that's correct. But without you questioning me and getting to the root, we wouldn't be here. Can you believe it? *Can you?* We are waiting for the movers to arrive... *Ahhhhhh!*"

Diana now lives in Florida. Five words I write with pure joy. *Diana now lives in Florida.*

Although I am beyond excited to have her in the same state as me now, I am more excited about the work she did to get here. I am more excited that she chose herself and her family, her Fab Four unit, and put them at the top of her list. That her values now align with the life she is creating. That while some of her deepest fears did become a reality (she has been called selfish and self-serving), despite the reactions and inactions of others, she did it anyway.

You see, lassies and lads, Diana living in Florida is beautiful, yet it took choosing to UnFollow many years of people-pleasing, specifically parent-pleasing and good-girl attitudes, to make it happen. Sometimes, when we do the work, our fears become a reality. And yet, as I told Diana, you move, and they could say those words; you stay put, and they could say those words, too.

Diana didn't move to spite people, but in spite of people.

We UnFollow not to spite people, but in spite of people.

Diana lives in Florida because she allowed that quiet inner knowing that was nudging her inside to *roar*. She allowed that little eight-year-old girl inside her to know, "I got this. Forty-year-old Diana has got this." That is the real work she did.

That deep desire to please becomes our shield when we are little. Sometimes, we spend our whole life acting like we still are.

At the beginning of some keynote speeches I give, I bring out a baby doll. I tell my audience she is me at eight years old. Taped to her little cabbage-doll body is a photo of me at eight years old. I ask the crowd if someone will hold her for me, as she is very worried to speak in front of a large crowd of people.

"She is scared you won't like what I have to say and that people might laugh at us."

The crowd laughs, and then someone always raises their hand, and they keep her for the whole speech. You see, thirty-eight-year-old Melissa has got this. She can do this. She has spent years watching TED Talks and working with a speaking mentor to master her craft, so, actually, thirty-eight-year-old me is pretty darn good at it now. And yet, if I allow eight-year-old Melissa to run the show, I get nervous. I take out jokes, I tone down my energy and my sarcastic humor, and I soften the blow of a message that requires a love punch.

Thirty-eight-year-old Coach Mummabear *Roars*. She doesn't speak softly, she drops some occasional inappropriate language for comedic effect, and she changes lives in the crowd.

Forty-year-old Diana is amazeballs. A bad mamma jamma. A move maker. A life shaker. She is now sending me pics of her kids and her at the beach a few minutes from their new home, at the neighborhood play area, and from her pool, where her kids are jumping around in the background. She is calling me from her new home office and planning for her sister and brother to visit. Forty-year-old Diana is self-assured. Forty-year-old Diana lives for her core Fab Four. Forty-year-old Diana knows her values and lives them. She isn't just roaring; she *is* the Roar!

"I'm framing it," Diana said.

On the video coaching call, she held up a Post-it I had her write. It says, *I live in Florida.*

"Matt is buying me a frame, and it's going on my office wall. What should we do next?" she asked.

We both laughed. But we were serious.

The "Power of the Post-it" is a term I coined. I branded some Post-its with my MelissaWiggins.life logo, made by my amazing and talented friend/brother from another mother, Rich Johnson. I have my clients write their goals on them like they are already done. Writing it like it's already done is a vital part of the process. It's pushing into belief. And the bonus comes when you see it daily, as it programs it in into your subconscious. Remember, our most practiced thoughts become our beliefs, and our beliefs become our perspective, and our perspective becomes our reality.

"I know for sure, what we dwell on, is who we become."
—Oprah Winfrey

That night after we sat in the woods, Diana showed me her Post-it. She had written it like it was already done: *I live in Florida.* She placed it in plain sight, to see it every day in her office in New Jersey. The power of visualization, coupled with belief in self, is the true Power of the Post-it. The power of curiosity. The power of you. The power of exciting questions.

ONE.Life, lassies and lads. What are you going to do with it? Eighty-year-old you is counting on you—make her or him proud.

Choosing to UnFollow parent-pleasing is similar to unfollowing people-pleasing, but it's something that is talked about way less. In fact, I am not sure I have ever heard anyone talk about parent-pleasing. The problem is, most of my clients, along with my friends and I, have all dealt with this, and some of us always will. How many times have you heard, "Oh, I will move when my parent passes away." How many of us in our thirties, forties, and fifties are still living to please our parents? We might not think of it in this way and instead live in justification of our actions.

We love our parents—most of us—but we get confused between loving and pleasing.

Love is unconditional. It's a bond; it's two-sided. Pleasing is conditional. It's not a bond; it's one-sided. Yet, many of us dare not rock the boat. We dare not attempt to move to a two-sided equation. That feels like we are renegotiating the contract.

But what if that's what it takes, lassies and lads? What if this is our season to renegotiate the unwritten contracts of our eight-year-old self and show up differently, so that our eighty-year-old self is proud of us someday?

If my kids say they won't move out-of-state, go abroad, not take a job/take a job because of *me*, I will feel like I failed them. I failed my job. My job is to allow my children the space to *know* themselves and pursue their dreams.

When I see kids go to college close to their parents, I wonder if that's because they worry about their parents, instead of listening to their inner knowing that's whispering "Alabama, Roll Tide," or whatever school you should choose. Of course, if you enjoy winning, Alabama is definitely a great choice. Also, if you're wondering how a lassie who attended law school in Scotland became an Alabama fan, you will need to keep reading.

Often, our pleasing of our parents started innocently on both sides. No one was trying to harm anyone, and no one was even aware of the harm. The reason I call this work "data collecting" is this is not the time to put blame on our parents or ourselves. But it *is* the time to question everything with excitement. The *UnFollow* method is a way of life. It leads you to not living your best life or being your best self, but to living your favorite life, your ONE.Life.

I've witnessed lassies in their eighties still concerned with their fathers' opinion of them, to the extent they almost kill themselves, taking care of their elderly parent. I've coached a fifty-year-old client through role play on how to approach her seventy-year-old mother about a renegotiation of the terms of their unwritten contract. I've coached a client who refused to talk about her mother, despite a decade of therapy around the issues the relationship had created, and then she finally talked about her mother and completely renegotiated their entire relationship.

Often, these shifts are met with disdain and disapproval. They are unwanted, judged, shamed, or branded as selfish. Yet, if we stay the course, if we UnFollow long enough to have the discomfort of change be outrun by the joy of inner knowing, an EMPOWERED.Life awaits us.

This work is not for the faint of heart. It's often avoided; some of us only see it or do it much later in life. Yet, it could be the most significant work of your ONE.Life.

Let's choose to question everything with excitement, like Diana did. This will be the journey to *Follow* Your Inner Knowing, and it might be the most exciting yet.

❦

THE WORK

Follow Your Inner Knowing

*"Don't let the noise of others' opinions drown out
your own inner voice."*
—Steve Jobs

o What quiet nudge inside you needs to be a ROAR?
o What could you do to make your eight-year-old and eighty-year-old self proud?
o What areas of your life do you need to tell your eight-year-old inner child to sit down and that you've got this?
o The Power of the Post-it: What goals can you write like they're already done and put on a Post-it to keep in plain sight? What do they say?
o What do you need to *UnFollow* in spite of people, not to spite people?
o Whose disapproval scares you the most?
o What does your favorite version of you say to your parents?
o What does your favorite version of your life sound like?
o Write your intentions around this work.
    Example: Intention—I am willing to sit in the uncomfortable process to *UnFollow* in order to get comfortable with my inner knowing.

CHAPTER 11

UnFollow Boundary Blowups

*"You teach people how to treat you by what you allow,
what you stop, and what you reinforce."*
—Tony Gaskins

"**H**ey, did you know you can now mark your texts as unread?" my client, business partner, and friend, Brian bragged.

"Shut your face. You lie," I retorted.

"For real. Just swipe left, and it gives you the option on the text. What a great day."

Brian is busy. He is super-Type A, which is why we instantly hit it off. He also has a massive heart and has been on my nonprofit's board forever.

My excitement about marking read texts as unread piqued my curiosity.

I thought back to the time when I asked my mentor a question, and she responded to me simply, "No."

Rude, I thought. But after doing THE WORK, that is no longer my first thought. Just a friendly reminder:

"No is a complete sentence."
—Anne Lamott

A version of me once used to text back something along these lines,

Oh, I wish. I actually can't. I already have plans that night which I can't change, but please keep me in mind for next time. So sorry.

Today's version probably writes something like this:

No, I can't. Thanks for thinking of me.

Texting: it's like email on steroids. We live in a society that expects answers back as soon as they see *read* on the text. I am not immune from this thinking, but I am also uber-aware of the dangers of this thinking.

People-pleasing and boundaries are like the ugly sisters in *Cinderella:* they go hand-in-hand, and one cannot be handled without the other.

I have made a few rules for myself. I love rules. Rules are my boundaries. They are for me, not you. The number-one misconception about boundaries is that they are put in place to stop others from doing something. The hard facts are these: a boundary should not be like an electric fence. It is not designed to keep others out. A boundary is about you and for you, period. It is designed to allow you to live within your values, like a set of bylaws for your ONE.Life. (I am sorry for the legal terms. I continue to work to UnFollow the lawyer inside of me, but progress, not perfection, right?)

My mentor has boundaries. The bylaws of her life are not over-explaining herself or using her energy to justify her decision. It is, after all, her decision. Therefore, "No" was her answer.

My bylaws include never saying yes straight away, when asked if I will do something. This particular bylaw is because I am an easily excitable person. My answer will always be yes, but my answer should not always be yes.

This brings me to this question: why is it so hard to hear *no* and say *no?*

I am about to say something that could change your life forever. You may want to grab a cup of tea and get a soft blanket. People-pleasing and saying yes to others in fear of their reaction are actually manipulations. *Ughhh.* I know it's gross and hard to hear. *But,* people-pleasing is a kind way of saying, "Hi, I agree with you only so you will like me. I am a manipulator. Nice to meet you."

Harsh, I know. My clients call these love punches, but I share this because I've been given this love punch by my mentor, and it changed everything for me.

What if we say "sharing a boundary" instead of "setting a boundary?"

What if an EMPOWERED.Life means we don't set boundaries with someone, but instead we share our boundaries with them?

You are simply sharing your values and bylaws with another human. You are not setting them, because that implies that boundaries are different and changeable, depending on the circumstances, and that is not what a boundary is.

Us Type-A lassies and lads want to be liked. We want to be seen as flexible yet hard working, and smart yet funny. So, we bend. We manipulate. Which is why we get excited about unread text options, because with this we don't have to worry about over-explaining and pleasing and boundary-sharing. We simply make it unread and pretend we haven't read it yet. Except, we *have* read it, which leads to an uneasy feeling in us, as now we know, at some point, we have to respond.

Most of my clients early on in our work have one or two boundary issues that need to be addressed. The good news is, six to twelve months into this work, it's much less of an issue and definitely uses way less brain energy. The initial shock of this work is some of the hard conversations that need to be had with people, who will be shocked or impacted by your shared boundary.

Claire is sober. Her mother-in-law lives in town and is a daily drinker. Sometimes, she just randomly pops over without a call or text and shows up to see *her* grandkids. If this is a familiar feeling, lassies and lads, take comfort in knowing almost everybody is in need of mother-in-law or father-in-law uncomfortable boundary conversations. But, sadly, most of us mere mortal humans end up with boundary blowups instead of boundary blessings.

An EMPOWERED.Life is a result of choosing to *UnFollow* manipulation to be liked and instead choosing to *Follow* sharing your boundaries.

I would like to know if you have any guns in the house, and if so, are they locked away? I also don't allow drinking alcohol around my children and need to know if this will be happening in your home," I text.

My pre-teen son is devastated. "You did not just write that, Mum."

"Oh, but I did, son."

"Mummmmmmmmm."

"Sooonnnnnnnnnn."

My children continue to wish for a "cool" mum, and I continue to wonder if the discomfort of parenting a pre-teen will ever end. We are both hopeful.

My asking about guns and alcohol has zero to do with the actual family seeking to host my son, but it has everything to do with me sharing my boundaries. If I was boundary-setting, the rule would change, family to family. It doesn't. It's me, sharing a bylaw of my family. As a sober mum who has never had her children exposed to drunk people, it is something important to me, based on my values.

A boundary blowup would look like me not sharing this ahead of time, my preteen coming home to share that the parents were drunk and fell down on the floor, and he felt unsafe. Then ensues the full-on "Mummabear mode," which would most likely result in my child never being at the friend's house again, and most likely the end in their friendship.

What if boundary sharing is the easier, softer way instead of a boundary blowup? There was initial discomfort in texting the above, but this initial discomfort was like having your car serviced, so it didn't break down. You don't really want to book the appointment, you don't really want to be car-less for a day while they look at fifty ways to charge you a few thousand dollars to have your car deemed "road safe," yet you do it and save yourself a call to AAA Roadside Assistance.

Note that I don't share with the family that I'm fourteen years sober and grew up around falling-down-drunk people, and it scared me. Then, I became a fall-down-drunk lassie, and drunk people trigger me to no end. Nope. Here's to growth. Just sharing a boundary and not overexplaining. This is progress.

My clients ask me often, "How will I know if I'm growing?"

Many of us look for *Big, Bold, Neon Signs* saying, *YES! You're growing.* We look for big wins and huge shifts. Yet I have found my personal biggest growths, and that of my clients, come from noticing shifts like this. Sharing a boundary without explanation. These are the mini-magical moments.

We don't start there, lassies and lads. I never did, and neither do my clients. We start with loving the idea that we can quickly put texts back to unread. Growth is a journey, and it has taken me years to get to that text above, which I sent to Cannon's friend's parent. I am constantly encouraging my clients to be patient, and they will see and feel changes, but it takes time.

Claire's journey began with us creating scripts for how the conversation would go. I would be the mother-in-law and she would be her. I would pretend I was upset with her for sharing her boundary. She would get upset even practicing it. Then, one day, Claire experienced what I like to call the Power of the Group.

As someone who has sat in recovery meetings on a white plastic chair in a circle for over fourteen years, no one can convince me otherwise, there is absolutely such a thing as the power of a group. It is why I created ONE.Life, my monthly group-coaching subscription. This program is a hybrid of group and one-on-one coaching with me or my certified coaches. Many lassies refuse to do group coaching, thinking they get more from just one-one-one with me. It's a false notion, and here is why.

I watched Claire share her script with the group. We role-played in front of eight other lassies and lads.

Then, someone in the group said, "So, when are you doing this?"

Claire got nervous and said, "Well... Well..."

The other group member said, "How about we set a date and time?"

On our group page, Claire shared she'd set the date with her mother-in-law. Everyone cheered her on. The morning of the boundary sharing, the group encouraged her, keeping her accountable while supporting her with their, "You've got this!" posts.

That afternoon, she shared that she'd done it—and the cheering continued. The entire group was with her in spirit, and what happened is what I like to call "boundary blessings."

Boundary blessings are the opposite of boundary blowups. In order to have boundary blessings, you need to do the work. The work that Claire did. Claire experienced the collective power of a group of lassies and lads behind her. For over a decade, she had replayed this boundary-sharing conversation in her head, and yet never had the words come out of her mouth.

Boundary blessings are the results of the work. They do not mean you get the response you hope for or the one you dread. They mean *you* cleaned up your side of the street and you moved toward an EMPOWERED.Life, knowing you get ONE.Life. You became responsible for your ONE.Life. You stopped the blame game, and you freed up so much mental energy, knowing you were honest—not people-pleasing, not manipulating to be liked.

For a decade, Claire dreaded the doorbell, dreaded the impact of a drunk mother-in-law, and spent so much energy avoiding any type of conflict around it. She even went out of town on holidays, to remove the chances of a drunk pop-in.

This work changes the quality of your day-to-day life, but it also makes you feel strong and brave and aligned in your values. It's an example to others around you, whether a group like Claire or your kids are watching. This work matters, and so do you.

Claire started to focus on the excitement of blessings that would happen in her ONE.Life with this work. She started to question everything with excitement, knowing what was waiting for her on the other side of her discomfort was a truly aligned life and that favorite version of her ONE.Life was hers for the taking. And Claire took it.

?

THE WORK

Follow Boundary Blessings

---

*"Sometimes the most loving thing you can say is **no**."*
—Melody Beattie

o   Check your texts, what patterns do you see?

o   How could you honor your boundaries in responding to requests for your time?

o   List 3 responses or ways you will share your boundaries:

o   List 5 bylaws for your life, based on your values:

o   Write down a response that you fear hearing when you share your boundary.

o   Create a script for how you plan to respond when you feel your boundaries are being disrespected.

o   What conversation am I avoiding that will result in a boundary blowup, if not handled soon?

o   Who could I role-play this through with, before I have the conversation?

o   If I were writing a script about this, what would I say?

?

o What's one step I could take today to move toward sharing my boundaries?

o List 3 things that would stop you from sharing your boundary.

o List one boundary sharing that would change your entire life.

o List the boundary blessings that could come with this.

o Set a date and time to share a boundary.

CHAPTER 12

UnFollow Failure

"I never lose. I either win or learn."
—Nelson Mandela

I was driving to South Florida. Finally, it was time. I was excited, nervous. I called my sister.

"I am so freaking nervous and so freaking excited."

"Melissa. Mummabear! You have got this. You have worked so hard. So hard. And you have prepped your little face off. Not only that, your pitch is killer," my sister said, trying to calm me down.

I knew my elevator pitch like I know my kids, inside out. And I was ready. She was right. It was time to swallow that little bit of sick in my throat and man up—or woman up? Boss up? Whatever the cool kids say. It was time. This moment.

I met my business partner in the hotel lobby. We went over everything one last time.

"You are so ready."

He asked me some questions, and I killed the answers. We got this.

I went to bed feeling prepared. I slept well. Jumped out of bed at 4 a.m., got ready, and headed to the TV recording studio.

I was about to pitch on live TV for a product I was the co-creator of. As a serial high performer and entrepreneur, I was jacked up—I'd never had this opportunity. I also love being on a team, and I wanted to make the rest of the team so proud.

My entrepreneur life began selling sweets (candy) in my garden (backyard)at the age of ten. Listen, back in the day, kids didn't do lemonade stands every three minutes. I was basically the OG of this, and us nineties kids, we didn't get no five pounds or five bucks for one cup of homemade lemonade. Oh, no. We had to work a little harder, lassies and lads. I had my savings, and my parents took me to Cash and Carry, basically a mini-version of Costco. *Where are my Costco people?* I would buy in bulk then make hot chocolate and sell candy, therein beginning my journey.

I was the one to go to for the good stuff. Everyone knew to walk back to my little wooden treehouse my dad had built me. This thing was legit: it had real windows and little curtains and electricity, and I loved it. I had the bug.

Now, thirty years later, there I was, no longer the girl from Irvine, who grew up in council housing (government housing). *No.* I was legit. I was about to go on TV and pitch for hundreds of thousands of dollars for our company.

I wasn't allowed to tell anyone about the show, as it had to be a secret. Same thing when Netflix wanted me as a life coach on a TV show, to work with the star of a reality show. It was all very top-secret.

The way this show worked was you had two minutes— yes, *two*, lassies and lads, to pitch your wee arse off.

Funnily enough, this wasn't my first pitch for two minutes. A few years back, in front of 1000 guests, I pitched for two and a half minutes about our nonprofit, Cannonball Kids' cancer. The guests voted their favorite pitch of all ten nonprofits. The winner won $25,000 for their nonprofit. This was a huge deal, and in Central Florida, this was the Who's Who and, well, it felt pretty major. I won, and our nonprofit got the money.

But this? This was three celebrity judges, all bazzilionares from their entrepreneur successes, and this was, hello, not 1,000 people but millions of viewers. Did I mention the seventy-five cameras and the lights that looked like a Disney movie was about to be produced?

They got me into makeup and hair and by 6 a.m. I was ready to pitch. There were six of us pitching that day. Have you ever sat in a room of people who are all interviewing for the same job? That was kind of the feeling in the room. Everyone wanted to know about each other's product, and we cheered each other on as each person was taken out, one by one. Days went by. Okay, not days, but seriously... days.

You never got to see anyone after they pitched live to the judges. They were escorted through different doors by different people. They did this on purpose. They told us as they did not want us to talk to each other or give tips or clues on how to act, be, pitch, etc.

A TV crew came and took us to a separate room and said, "Okay, this is for B-roll." For those of you who, like me, quickly Googled *B-roll*, this was the part where shows show a little about the people in the show. So, we Zoom called my four kids, who were perfectly dressed and perfectly behaved, sitting on my favorite green-velvet sofa in my homemade studio in my house. (It's a guest bedroom—don't get too excited). There may have been some serious bribing done to make this a reality, but there sat my four perfect children, and they raved about our product and smiled and joked with the TV crew.

My clan of kids are fun, and they were born for TV, but me? *Me?* I was getting a little more nervous now. It was the waiting. *Ugggghhhh.*

I waited thirteen hours. Thirteen hours is how long I waited for my son to come out of surgery to remove his cancer at age two. He spent his second birthday on life support for five days. I reminded myself of this as I start to feel vomity— is that a word? But, vomity I felt.

"Melissa, this is not surgery, not your son. Although this product feels like a child of yours, it is not," I told myself to calm my wee nervous system.

One by one, they took away the others. Hours passed between each of them. And then, there I was, the only one sitting in the cold, very white cafeteria-like holding area.

Finally, a lassie with a headset and all kinds of things clipped to her body arrived. She was holding a walkie-talkie, and she radioed over to confirm she could bring me to a second holding room. Some eleven hours had passed now. The crew were beyond kind and gracious.

My brain said, "You're last—the celebs must be exhausted." I quickly "Thought Reset," a tool my clients love, and I'd developed because often my first thought isn't the best thought.

Did you know we have 60,000 thoughts a day? Did you also know eighty percent of them are negative? Ninety-five percent are the same as the day before. Hence why I developed this tool and trained my clients on it extensively. Anytime I develop a tool, I am the beta. So, there I was in this situation where my brain was going there.

What if?

What if it was actually a major win that you are last?

What if they are so excited about you being last, because they go home next?

Three or four people gathered in the hallway, and one of them summoned me to come. They put on my mic and took me to the elevator.

"You got this," they said, knowing I was vomity again.

The elevator didn't actually move, but we pretended it did, and a timer counted down from five. Someone yelled in the background, "*Quiet in the studio!*"

Everything was very quiet, which was crazy as there were some fifty people making this magic happen today.

Inside the elevator, it was very bright.

5, 4, 3, 2, 1.

The doors opened. Cameras. Light. A very loud voice said something over the whole studio, but I was in such a dissociative state, I didn't make it out.

Immediately, a timer started going down, down, down with the number of seconds left in my pitch. I had practiced on a camera and recorded and rewatched myself do this pitch

?

nine million times. No, really—okay, maybe eight million, but a lot.

Words were coming out of my mouth, but they weren't in the order I'd planned. *Crap.* I was bombing. I made a joke—my go-to in very awkward situations. A few more sentences came out of my mouth, but I couldn't tell you what they were. The doors closed again. The three celebs were in a studio a few hundred feet away, watching me. They decided whether they would open the doors again and let me in to fully pitch to them. It was not a given. Not everyone got through, and I knew this. *Hello*, I'd binged every episode of this show to get there.

By some miracle, a loud voice congratulated me, and the doors opened. I was escorted by three or four people to the next area, where our product was on display, and three celebrity judges would decide if they would invest in us. I so badly wanted this for the team—they had worked their arses off. I was a small cog in the wheel, but that day, I was there, trying to play big for all of them and their years and years of hard work.

Yet again, another elevator, and this time, the doors opened to three people sitting in chairs. Having studied the judges, I felt I knew enough about their paths to success, their mishaps, and their interests.

The doors opened and before I could open my wee Scottish gob, I was greeted with, "You're lucky you are here. We were not in agreement that you should be here. In fact, it was me who didn't want to let you come here and pitch to us. I don't even understand what you're pitching me. Your pitch was not clear. What exactly is it? Maybe you can change my mind, but right now, it's unlikely..."

Thirteen hours. So much vomity, and then *this*?

Holy Mother of Mary.

What could I say to this guy? Could I ignore him and maybe focus on the other two? They appeared to be smiling. In fact, the only women on the panel might have just winked at me.

Oh, she was so beautiful, winky and beautiful and brilliant and rich. Get it, lassie. Get it.

Somehow, words came out. "Well, I think once you hear about our patent-approved lid for our tumbler, I might be able to change your mind."

He interjected immediately. "I doubt it. I mean, are you a tea company or a tumbler company? What are you?"

I said something about how Scotland, my home country, actually popularized tea in the 1600s, and I grew up making it for my family. It was a tradition at home.

"Yes, but what is it?"

"Could I have you come to the presenting table, and I'll show you?"

Instantly, the camera men signaled to me they cannot leave the chair area right now, due to camera locations. The interruption surprised me, and I lost my train of thought. Questions were being fired at me like a one-year-old throws food off their high chair. I answered, and yet I felt like it was not hitting the mark. My answers felt weak, even to me.

They tried the tea and loved it. But it was not enough. All three said it's not for them until I had a more solid marketing plan. I did have a solid marketing plan, it was just my brain didn't say the words.

I thanked them all for their time.

Instantly, the cameras interviewed me about not getting a deal. I told them I would be back and this wouldn't be the last they'd see of me.

I felt so defeated. I cancelled dinner with my business partner, went to the hotel, and packed up. I didn't care if I got home at midnight, I wanted to be in my own bed and see my babies.

My business partner placated me with some words, but none of it did much to help. I called my sister and told her it was the hardest thing I'd ever done. That I'd bombed and didn't get a deal, and whoopee, it would be on TV. I professionally catastrophized and got off the phone.

When I watched the show when it was released, it was even more painful than the thirteen hours. One of the judges actually got off the chair—they must have changed cameras by then—and stood beside our table set up. He pretended to pitch our product while he and the other judges laughed. He mocked me, and everyone laughed. Sigh.

Why do I share this? I made a promise to myself a few years ago that part of my role in this ONE.Life is to share the messy middle.

Sharing the messy middle is an act of rebellion. It is a stepping stone to bravery.

At eleven years sober, I first shared my sobriety story. Eleven. Eleven years of secrecy. But the truth is, at age twenty-five, I didn't have the tools to be brave enough to share my messy middle. The thoughts of "What if I tell people, then I drink?" consumed me too much.

While I would love to share that the pitch got us a million-dollar deal and our Bruetta Tea tumbler is now on every retail shelf in America, with our tea now stocked at Starbucks—that's not where we are. It doesn't mean it's not where we're going, but that's not where we are. That doesn't mean we are losing; it means we are learning.

They are not so shiny or glam, the middle parts of the story. So often, we see the start and then "*boom!*", success. But in my experience, that often isn't how it goes.

The messy is about changing the status quo. It is about moving closer to living vulnerably and authentically, so others can be inspired to do so, too. We live in a world of, "I am great. How are you?" and yet suicide is at an all-time high.

What if our generation's act of rebellion is less about sharing our winnings and failures and more about our learnings? Our unlearning and relearning? Our UnFollowing.

What if this generation's job is to share the "to be continued...."

To be continued is that place where we just don't know how things will go, and we're okay with that. Being okay with progress and pattern shifts and the unknown. Sitting in the discomfort of that. There is wisdom there. What is yours? The research is clear—our messy middles, our "to be continued," are where we learn the most.

What if, instead of fear and shame of being in the messy middle, we had excitement? We had questions that inspired us to continue. To never quit. When we look at this season as winning and learning, it is exciting—full of possibility and hope. It's only when we stay feeling like we failed that we lose—truly lose. I don't know about you, lassies and lads, but I am not here to lose in this ONE.Life. My ONE.Life is for my clients, my family, and me to *live life to the fullest*.

By choosing to question everything with excitement, we move away from focusing on how it went, and instead, we focus on where we are going.

THE WORK
Follow Winning or Learning

*"The only real mistake is the one from which
we learn nothing."*

—Henry Ford

o Think of a time you felt like you failed:
  How could you thought reset that so-called failure into
  a win?
o How do you define winning?
o How do you define learning?
o My messy middle is:
  Describe the things you will learn from your messy
  middle:
o My favorite way I want my messy middle to conclude
  is:
o At the conclusion of my messy middle, I want to feel:
o I plan to show up for my messy middle like:
o What would my life coach tell me today about my
  messy middle?
o My "To Be Continued" is:
o If I did know how my "To Be Continued" would end, it
  would be:

CHAPTER 13

UnFollow Perfectionism

"Perfectionism is a twenty-ton shield that we lug around, thinking it will protect us, when, in fact, it's the thing that's really preventing us from taking flight."
—Brené Brown

A ll right, Mel. Wake up! It's 3 a.m."
I thought to myself, it can't be time to wake up. It can't be time to wake up. I just went to bed.

I was, of course, a teenage girl, but also a complete morning person. Not much has changed since then. And my siblings tease me for being a carbon copy of my dad.

My dad was a window cleaner when we were growing up, and I'd been cleaning windows with him since I was ten. I had my own little ladder, and I had my own belt with a squeegee and rags for cleaning the windowsills. I loved working. I especially loved working with my dad.

I will never forget our white bread with large blocks of cheese and butter sandwiches and some onion inside it—delicious. Always chased down with an incredibly warm cup of tomato soup, or sometimes, we mixed it up, with cream of chicken soup. Scotland is cold. Imagine dipping your hands in cold water and washing windows. Eating became our joy every day.

On Fridays, if we'd had a good week, meaning Dad was paid by people on time, we would buy our lunch. Greggs—#IYKYK. A large cheese softie and a cake. In Scotland, it rains a lot. So often, we got home, soaked to the bone. It didn't matter. My dad always went into his little hut at the back of the garden that he had made into a little workout gym, and he worked out for an hour.

"All right, Mel. Get out of the car. This is the place."

We started with the inside. It was a dreary building, probably an old 1980s sandstone, with what looked like two to three floors. We drove in on the stone driveway and unloaded our equipment. I had my window-cleaning belt on and was ready to go.

"What is this place, Dad?"

"Oh, this is a group home. These kids have been chucked out by their parents or have no parents."

"Hi, hen. Howwww you doing today?"

"Aye, greattt, pal."

In Scotland, we elongate our words. My dad and mum have never met a stranger in their life, so my dad's familiarity with the receptionists was just normal banter for him.

"All right, Mel, let's start upstairs."

There was dark-green carpet going up the stairs, and the walls were a little beaten up. This place was huge. As we got up to the second floor, I saw that there were a bunch of kids playing pool. I saw other kids bustling in and out of their rooms. They were my age, some younger, some older. My stomach started to get queasy. I was not a soft girl. I didn't cry. In fact, I didn't really start crying until my thirties... But more on that later.

We went into one of the bedrooms. The door was open.

"Hi, pals. How you doin'?" my dad said in his chirpy voice.

The kids smiled and left the room, so we could clean the window. The room was small and crammed with bunk beds, with very little floor space. The window was a tiny box window up very high. I later wondered if that was on purpose, so the kids didn't leave during the night. As a lassie who grew up in government housing and lived with my siblings in one room, in an upstairs apartment with one bathroom until I was high school, I felt for these kids.

We had recently been given a larger home for our family by the government—what is called council homes in Scotland. I now had my own room for the first time in my life. My room looked onto a beautiful golf course, and my windows were large and opened. I loved windows. I still love windows with a view. Not sure why a lassie who doubled as a window cleaner would love windows, but there's something satisfying about a clean window and something green outside—like a mural, but better. Real nature. This lack of view and window for these kids crammed into a room pained me. But not as much as the half-smile the kid gave my dad.

I am just as chirpy as my dad, and I started smiling at every kid I saw. It felt sad there. It felt lonely. Even as a teen, my empath/intuitive side could feel their sadness. There I was with my dad, working with him. I went home to my mum, who had created a beautiful clean home for us, with dinner on the table, and she would be standing at the door with a warm cup of tea as we came in. Government housing or not, I was the luckiest lassie alive, as I'd won the parent lottery. They cared for me, encouraged me, pushed me in sports and school, and they knew where I was and how I was getting home. They were present. But these kids—they had been rejected by their parents and society, and they didn't have someone giving them a warm cup of tea or a window with a view or a room to themselves.

Without being dramatic, but maybe you've already sensed my drama side from previous chapters, this day changed my whole life. My whole life. Tears roll down my face just writing this, thinking back to what it felt like in that group home, an orphanage for teens.

I didn't know for how many years this day and the subsequent days of cleaning this home would impact my soul, but it was inside me. I knew one day I would adopt. I would change one kid's life, a child like those kids inside that group home.

During my early sobriety, that impact looked like me taking on a one-year commitment. Every Friday night, I would go to the juvenile detention center and host a recovery meeting there, with a group of other incredible, sober women. It's so very easy to cast judgment on young offenders, but my heart says, if you only knew what they endure, the lack of love and support at such a vulnerable age, you may not be so judgmental. These teens would come out in jumpsuits and flip-flops, and some were handcuffed to tables. I would sit at the front of the room at age twenty-five, thinking of those lassies and lads from the group home.

"Hey, do you remember me?" a voice said.

I looked up from the sink where I was washing my hands. Truth be told, names and faces are a nightmare for me. I feel like I black out, when anyone asks me that, and internally, I hear, "Come on, Melissa. You got this, you got this."

I responded, "I am sorry, I don't. How do I know you?" She was beautiful, with long blonde hair, a slim build, and those soulful, piercing-blue eyes.

She laughed. "To be fair, I look very different than the last time you saw me."

I was in a bathroom with which I was very familiar. The flower wallpaper brought me comfort. I'd washed my hands in those sinks for fourteen years. Fourteen years of sober living. It was at a meeting I call my Home Group: a group I committed to every week. I attended business meetings, I stood at the door, and I greeted people. Every Thursday, 7 p.m., that was my location, unless I was out of town or couldn't get a sitter.

"You came to the juvenile detention center. You spoke, and you changed my life. I have been sober for a few years now."

I smiled, placed my hand on her arm, and told her the truth.

"No, beautiful lassie, you changed your life."

She teared up. We hugged, left the bathroom, and took our seats in the meeting room. During that whole meeting, I couldn't stop thinking about the group home. My promise to adopt.

My plan always was to adopt. When I met my husband, we talked about it in the first month of dating. That said, Cannon being far enough and safe enough away from his cancer journey was truly our focus. We needed to make sure his cancer would never come back and our kids were okay before pursing this.

The weeks following this meeting, I started having dreams about adopting. Frankly, it really irritated me. I would wake up having seen images of me adopting a little girl. She looked two or three years old. Over and over, the same dream. *But this was not the time.* I was the CEO of our nonprofit. At this time, I spent most of my life living out of a suitcase, traveling to hospitals around the world, finding innovative first-of-its-kind research for pediatric cancer, speaking on stages for funds, and at home with my incredible four-year-old twins, Arran and Gray, and a five-year-old Cannon.

One morning, after yet another dream, I was beyond irritated. I woke up, looked up to the ceiling, and said these words: *"Fine, God! Fine! You win.* I will call an adoption agency!"

I told my husband the hundred reasons this was not the right time. I told him the hundred reasons I couldn't do it right now. I told him the hundred reasons why I was too busy, as I had other focuses right now, I was tired, and we didn't have the money or resources. One hundred reasons for how I didn't know how to even start. (That one's funny, since I'd spent most of my life, from law school to kids' cancer research, figuring things out.)

The cold hard truth was this: I was allowing my perfectionist tendencies to once again rule my life and keep me from a life goal of mine.

The truth is I was asking all the wrong questions. Many of us are asking all the wrong questions.

What if we have a failed adoption? What if we are rejected, and we can't adopt? My husband was older; what if they don't let us? I was arrested at twenty-three for a DUI; what if they don't know I am sober now?

So, I began doing what I do best: researching massive amounts of information and finding solutions. I began to use the tools I had learned over the years to manage my mind and my day.

But more importantly, I started asking the right questions. I started asking questions that excited me, questions that had me visualizing this girl from my dreams in my family, at our dinner table, and with us on vacations. We even joked about where her car seat would go.

I decided to *Start Before I was Ready*.

Start Before You Are Ready

Start Before you are Ready looks like this:

The first thing I needed to do was let the board of the nonprofit my husband and I had founded know. I told them I had one year left as CEO, and since I had built the nonprofit from zero dollars to a million dollars raised in a year, I was ready to hand the position off to a professional nonprofit leader.

I had never wanted to be the CEO of our nonprofit. I had taken on the position to get us where we needed to be, but I built it knowing I could never stay in the pediatric cancer world every day. I have been to more kids' funerals than adults', and, as a mum who fought this war with her own son, every day was pretty traumatic at my job. I helped find my replacement, knowing that all the literature said a minimum of six months was required for an adopted child to bond with her adoptive parents. I wanted to give that gift of time to the little girl in my dream.

My husband and I began saving and putting away his bonuses, so we could handle the costs. Since I was still working as the CEO, I worked on the adoption every night after the kids were in bed. I started treating our adoption like it was my part-time job in the evenings. This is when I handled the paperwork side, which amounted to mountains of it. We read all the books on adoption and multiracial families. We attended seminars on biological kids and adoptive kids. *We got ready.*

Start before you are ready is all about action. Doing. It's about putting down the twenty-pound shield of perfectionism and saying, "I am doing this in spite of what might go wrong." It's stopping asking the questions that keep you stuck, in fear or shame, and instead start asking ones that get you excited and imagining your favorite version of your ONE.Life.

And things did *go wrong.*

So wrong.

But before that, many things went oh, so right.

I began praying that God would send me this big sign. A *huge* sign that I would know the right child for our family. That the sign was so big and so clear, there would be *no* mistake it was right for our family. My fear was I wouldn't be able to say no to a child the agency presented. Over and over, this was my prayer. *Sign! HUGE!*

"Can you call us this morning?"

That's all the email said. My stomach dropped a little. Could they be calling because they'd found a match? A match in the adoption world means, based on the social worker's recommendation and the needs of a child and the capacity of your family, they feel you are a good family match.

My husband and I wanted to keep the natural biological order of our family, so we were looking for a child aged two to five. No disrespect to the baby stage, but it was not my jam.

Could have been the three kids under age two and one with cancer—but it also could be I'm just not a baby-stage lover. So, ages two and above was our hope. Hubby wanted a five-year-old, and I wasn't far behind him.

As soon as I got to my office, I closed the door and went to the corner of the room, staring out the window at the other office buildings. I pressed dial, and every ringtone felt like an eternity.

"Hi, Melissa. It's Claudia and Nadia here."

"Hi, how are you?"

"We are so great. Is this a good time to talk?"

"Yes, yes, of course."

"We just got back from our trip to Medallion, Colombia, and we think we have a child for you. But before we send you a photo of her, we want to tell you some things about her."

The horrible part of adoption is that many countries desire perfect children—not sure what that means, since I've yet to meet one, but let's just say that vanity plays a role.

"It's a little girl. She is eighteen months old and was born October 14."

What?

"When was she born?"

"October 14, 2017."

My heart was racing. It was so fast, I felt like I couldn't catch my breath. My stomach is somersaulting, and I was having some kind of out-of-body experience.

Growing up, birthdays in my country were a huge deal; at least they were in my household. My thirty cousins and all my aunts and uncles and Gran and Papa would all come by the house with cards and money. Mum always made everything special, and birthdays were no different. She always woke us up with birthday cake and everyone singing to us. It was special then, and it's special now. I followed this tradition in my house, and birthdays of any age remain a huge deal.

"Wait, October 14?"

"Yes," Nadia replied.

"That's my birthday," I said. "That's my birthday."

The sign! I had asked God for a *huge* sign. A *big-deal* sign. Nothing small. Something big and glaring and knowing. Birthday twins? Really, God? Wow. You outdid yourself. The ladies went on to tell me she had been in the orphanage since she was nineteen days old. She was born addicted to drugs, and her birth mother's rights had been terminated.

My heart instantly ached for the little girl and for her mother. As someone who understands addiction and has been around it for many years and who, hello, is a recovering alcoholic—well, this also felt like a sign to me. Someday, I would be able to explain to that little girl that her mum loved her but was very sick.

Nadia said "The issue is she requires two huge surgeries. She has craniosynostosis, and that will require her to be opened up from ear-to-ear to have her skull fixed. She should have had this done as a newborn, but with the drug issues and the orphanage situation, it hasn't happened. As a result, one eye is higher than the other, and her head has grown in a funny shape."

Honestly, everything after the words *October 14* was a blur.

She told me she would send a photo and give me a week to decide.

In that week, I talked to all my neurosurgeon friends. Most of my friends are doctors, since my work at Cannonball Kids' cancer Foundation has primarily funded brain-cancer research in kids. I called my friend Gregor Alexander, who is one of the most well-known NICU doctors in the world; the hospital literally named the NICU unit after him. His research has pioneered so much change for NICU families.

Gregor said he knew the guy I needed to talk to. This guy was a neurosurgeon and world-renowned. "He is the one you want."

Day 5: I found myself sitting in a parking lot, waiting for the neurosurgeon's call.

"Melissa, Gregor told me I had to call you. Any friend of Gregor's is a friend of mine," Dr. Alababa said. "I've reviewed the files you sent me in Spanish." (Everything was in Spanish, and guess who could speak and read Spanish? Correct, Dr Albaba.)

Then, he uttered four words that changed everything.

"I *can do it.* I can have her in and out in a week. We will need a plastic surgeon, along with me, since it's her head and face, but I can fix this. It's going to take two surgeries, six months apart. All you have to do is go get that little girl from Colombia and let me know when you land in the U.S."

Be still my soul.

Nine hundred calls with insurance later (thank you, husband—not my strong suit), we knew we could get her added to our insurance.

Day 6: My husband came up behind me and hugged me while I stared at her photo. He said, "I don't know." My heart sank. "She is younger than we agreed on, and we said no huge medical issues, since we just spent three and a half years fighting stage 4 cancer with our son."

He was right; we did agree on those terms. Something told me to leave it. Let him be. If this was to be our daughter, he would come around. Me persuading him was not part of the deal.

Day 7: I had a call scheduled with Nadia and Claudia that morning at 9 a.m.

That morning, Michael came up to me and said these words, which I will never, ever forget; the kindest, most beautiful words he has ever uttered to me in our twenty years together.

"I trust you. I trust you with our life and our family, and if you believe this is our daughter, then let's do it."

In the coming months, I flew to Medellín with my friend, Maria Basso. Maria is from South America, and Spanish is her first language. She loves Colombia and agreed to come with me.

The agreement with the orphanage was that Maria and I were volunteers. I must not in any way act as if I were her mother. During our stay in Colombia, I visited many places that helped children there. But the day we went to the orphanage will be a part of my core memories for life.

There were fifty kids in this orphanage, each of them waiting for a family—abandoned, rejected, unwanted—just like the group home where my dad and I window-cleaned.

When we toured it, I got to see where she slept. Some twenty-plus cribs crammed into one room. This was her life. This was her norm. This was all she had known for twenty months of her life. Twenty months of sharing a room with twenty babies. Twenty months of different caretakers. Twenty months of living in this house.

They took us to a room that had nowhere to sit. It was just a concrete floor. About ten different kids ran into the room, and every single kid was obsessed with me. They wanted attention and hugs and for Maria and me to play with them. Except one. Which one would you think that is, if you had to guess? Yup. *That* one. The one I was there for.

A caretaker sat on the ground with the little girl from my dreams between her legs. She was crying and so upset, she didn't want anything to do with me. The caretaker pointed to her eye and head and gave me a look that said, "Do you see it?"

Internally, I thought, *Yes, of course I see it. Her one eye is much higher than the other and her head is very deformed.*

I looked into the little girl's eyes, and I loved her so much. This was my daughter. I loved her no matter what she looked like or what she needed. She was my daughter, and I was her mother.

The caretaker nudged me again, pointing to the area. I was unphased, and she was confused. Perhaps it was three and a half years of cancer treatment with my son or the many kids' funerals that made me this way, but either way, it didn't scare me, not one bit.

Then, someone came in and yelled something in Spanish. Instantly, my girl got up and ran to the door. Maria nudged me. *It's lunch.* I giggled a little. My girl was a foodie, just like me and her dad.

I watched in amazement as these little one- and two-year-olds took their seats at the table and prepared for lunch.

They served arroz and pollo. My girl was using a fork, and her manners were impeccable. I thought to myself, *What in the world? My boys were not doing this at age twenty months.'*

My girl still wanted nothing to do with me. Every other kid, yes. Her, no.

It's okay, I thought, food is my life. I got this. I started pretending I was going to eat some off her fork. She giggled, then instantly realized she'd let her guard down and became serious.

I tried again. She giggled. But now, she started using the fork and pretending she was going to give some to me, and just as I went to take a bite, she snatched it away and stuffed it in her mouth. The giggles ensued. That was how our love affair began. It began over chicken and rice.

I left Colombia with a piece of my heart in an orphanage. Six months later, my husband and I returned.

I wish this part of the story was joyful, but it wasn't. It was painful. Heart-wrenching.

Part of starting before you are ready means being comfortable with the uncomfortable. This is where true growth, resilience, and character-building are formed. It is not from the safe havens of our homes, but out in the wild.

Upon landing in Medellín, we received a call. The call crushed my soul.

The agency we were with lost their ability to do international adoptions. Apparently, this happened to a bunch of agencies all at the same time. As a result, they couldn't do what was needed in Colombia in terms of paperwork for us to get everything approved by the judge to adopt our girl.

"I think you should just go home to America," they said. "You won't be getting her."

By this point in the book, I feel like you know me well enough to know I did *not* get back on a plane and go home to Orlando.

No, no, no, I thought. This is not going to be one of those nightmare adoption stories that I'd completely deleted from my brain since the start of the process.

The days that followed were some of the hardest of our life. Ten days of little to no sleep, calls to political members with pull, and calls to other adoptive parents, to other agencies. I was relentless. I argued, fought, cried, and fought again. But nothing was working.

It became clear that the only path through was to ditch our agency and find another one while in Medellín. Heartbreaking, since I loved those lassies. They had found Charlie and they'd matched us, but decisions, the right and big decisions, are rarely easy.

Big decisions that are right are rarely easy.

After hundreds of hours of research and call after call, I finally found an agency willing to help us. It would cost us, and things would be tight, but we had saved so hard to make this happen that we would do anything to bring our lassie home.

Questioning everything means taking responsibility for your ONE.Life and your people.

Had I just gone home, life would be very different. The whole reason for this book is so you, the reader, question everything. Every single thing. I know lassies and lads who would have believed the agency, when they said go home, and they would have gone home. They would have booked their flight and headed back with no child. Why?

Many of us don't question things. We accept them as people tell us. I do not believe the agency was ever malicious in their intent, but I do believe, had I just done what they said,

? 131

I was handicapping my own capabilities, my own intuition, and my own wisdom. My own brain. My own resilience that had led me there. I think some of you reading this are doing the same, and I want to help you stop this. The entire purpose of this book is to develop the muscle of your inner knowing.

Many of us have outsourced our brains to others, thinking everyone else knows better than we do. It's false, and it's stunting our societal growth.

It was not an easy road. It was not. But I believe every single one of you has what it takes inside you. Most of you are scared to let out that inner Roar, but what if you did?

What if you said, "*No*, I am not going home."

Perfectionism

In all my work with my clients, the biggest issue I see people face is perfectionism. Perfectionism is so deeply misunderstood. Many of us wear it as a badge of honor, believing it means doing things perfectly. Perfectionism is so much deeper than doing things perfectly.

> "*Continuous improvement is better than delayed perfectionism.*"
> —Mark Twain

And yet, what I see over and over is procrastination—the ugly cousin of perfectionism.

My clients come to me thinking they are lazy or can't get it together or aren't focused. It's false advertising, and it's wrong. What they really have is a thought error in their minds. The thought that, if I look perfect, I can avoid disappointment, embarrassment, and save face. And what it's really doing is sabotaging their lives.

The ripple effect of this chronic error-thinking is we look for others to be perfect, too, to live up to this ideal we have in our brains. So, we judge them, and we judge us, and we stay stuck. "It's safe here," we tell ourselves.

Perfectionism is a thought error. What it's really doing is sabotaging our lives, keeping us stuck and procrastinating our potential.

Our most practiced thoughts become our beliefs. So, as we practice this thought error over and over, we begin to believe it. If ninety-five percent of what we do is in our subconscious, then the majority of our decisions and actions we just accept; most of our behaviors and emotions, we just do. On average, we

> **Perfectionism is a thought error.**

have 60,000 thoughts a day, and ninety-five percent of those are repetitive thoughts from the day before. Eighty percent of them are negative thoughts.

Have you ever brushed your teeth, got in your car, drove to work, and then wondered how you got there? Our subconscious drives the minivan, while our conscious mind is the little toddler kicking the back of our seat, saying, "Are we there yet?"

So often, then, we don't even know or see how our thoughts become our beliefs. We just do what we always do, and this feels like we are keeping ourselves safe.

We have 60,000 thoughts a day—60,000 sentences in our mind!

Our most practiced thoughts become our beliefs.

Eighty percent of our thoughts are negative.

Ninety-five percent of our thoughts are repetitive.

Identifying our own thought errors can be tough at first, but with practice, you will start to notice them come up. When you do, it's time to use a tool I created for my clients: the Thought Reset.

(Side note: this episode of my podcast, *Coaching and a Cup of Tea with Mummabear*, is the most listened to.)

Thought Reset is yet another tool inspired by my children. This one is inspired by Gray Roland Wiggins.

Early on, in my parenting journey, I wanted my kids to know that a bad morning didn't mean a bad day, that we had the power to restart our day at any time. One day, my sweet son, who for the first seven years of his life required everyone to call him Dr. Gray and even wrote this on his homework sheets, drew me a picture. The picture said *RESET* in big letters, with a sunbeam all around it.

Now, I want to be clear: I am the mum who is the opposite of a hoarder. Not sure

> **Our most practiced thoughts become our beliefs.**

what the modern world would call that, but I trash everything. I hate clutter, and I do not have seventeen drawings by my kids on my fridge. In fact, many times, I have been caught by my kids, when they find their work and drawings in the trash.

This drawing was different. I instantly found a frame for this one, and it has sat in our kitchen, in the most walked-past area of our home, for five years now. We press it as our magical button to reset our day, when we've had a bad moment or I have accidentally fallen off the beam and yelled or the kids have had a fight.

So, I started thinking about what my clients struggle with and decided they and I needed a thought-reset tool. A tool that allowed us to catch our thought errors and reset them instantly. It's funny now, in group coaching calls, sometimes my clients call me out and ask me to reset a thought.

Here are two of my personal thoughts that have needed resetting:

Marriage is hard.
Thought reset: Marriage requires watering, like anything you want to grow.

Being a mum is hard.
Thought reset: When I take care of my insides, being a mum feels so much more fun.

Okay, so you're reading this and thinking, "Really?" I liked this lassie, and now she is royally ticking me off with her positive psychology, mindset work.

Well, get in line, lassies and lads—you and every other client I coach.

I always Follow up with asking my clients this: *Is the thought true?*

And often, my clients feel like it is. Often, marriage and kids feel hard. It does. *But* the next question is how I plan to challenge you skeptics, and how I bring my clients, back to the work.

Is it helpful?

Is the thought helpful to my goals and my ONE.Life?

Marriage is hard! Kids are hard! May feel true. *But* is it helpful? Often the answer is no. It's not. So, I ask for a thought reset.

Being aware of your thoughts takes work. It takes practice. You may like what you find, and you may not. As a helpful tool for some thoughts that are common and require resetting, The Thought Reset exercise is available at melissawiggins.life.

Without tools like this, it can be easy to believe everything we think. *Don't!* Our brains are liars.

I could have believed what the adoption agency told me. I could have left Colombia without my daughter. I could have allowed my thoughts to remain in fear and lack of hope. By using the Thought Reset tool I developed, I was able to start asking myself exciting questions that helped me visualize the little girl from my dreams with our family. Exciting questions that change how our brain thinks. It retrains us to live our ONE.Life with more joy and hope.

Perfectionism will steal the life you deserve from you, and it will do it with no regrets.

The counter-action to this is, Start Before you are Ready. Focusing on what your future self would do, imagining the result you want, and doing it all before you are ready.

THE WORK

Follow Start Before You Are Ready

o   The three thought errors I keep having right now are:

o   Three thought resets to those thoughts are:

o   I define perfectionism as:

o   I see my perfectionism is holding me back in these 3 areas:

o   I can see I am procrastinating in these 3 areas:

o   One area I plan to focus on for the next year is:

o   The one thing I plan to Start Before I am Ready is:

o   The first step I will take to start that one thing is:

o   I will begin the one thing _____date, time

o   List three times you have done something someone suggested without questioning it.

o   What will you do next time and why?

o   Next time someone metaphorically tells you to go home, what will you do?

CHAPTER 14

UnFollow Raising Spoiled, Entitled Brats

"Never do for a child what he can do for himself."
—Elizabeth Hainstock

While I could have brainstormed a better *UnFollow* chapter title, because you know this title is one of the biggest fear of almost all parents. That their sweet child of Christ is a spoiled, entitled brat. Man, do we all know them. *Brat* felt kinder than some of the other words I word-smithed, though. You're welcome.

The straw that broke the camel's back: after an adventure week at the beach—note, I don't say *vacation* at the beach. The beach with kids is not a vacation, and anyone who says it is, is blasphemous.

As we got home and the entire car needed to be unpacked, the cooler and beach chairs, suitcases and snacks, I watched my littles get out of the car and go sit on the sofa, watching the TV. Internally, I lost it. I told my husband we were teaching them this was how family should be: where parents do all the work, and teamwork doesn't exist.

Ask Granny Bel—my mum, the greatest mum who ever lived—what her biggest parenting regret is (and the girl's got experience; she was a SAHM to five bairns). Granny Bel would tell you her regret was not including her kids in the operation of running a family home.

When I say Granny Bel did all the things for all the people, it's not my Scottish exaggeration-gene talking. We didn't clear our plates or do our laundry. We came home from school to beds made and home-cooked meals, and lunches always were packed for us. We watched TV on Sunday nights together, while my mum stood for twelve hours ironing all our clothes, only to find them in a pile in our room days later. We watched as she unloaded groceries, and let's just say, there was no fair play in our house. My job was my studies and my sport.

Problem: I decided to be a great daughter. (Hello, firstborn mindset here.) I would help do a laundry load for my mum. I'd watched her do this, as I told her all about my awful boyfriend, whom I loved and hated every other day. How hard could it be?

I set the number to 1, and I proudly walked away. I went back a few hours later and noticed the dial had moved to number 5. Dear God. I turned the number back to 1 and continued with my carefree teenage life, only to return to the same situation, back at number 5.

My Aunt Chic popped in, as she often did. I grew up with my aunties and uncles all in a two-mile radius. Aunt Chic was my bestie—she was so cool, and I told her everything. Everything I didn't tell my mum. Now that I am an adult and not a carefree teen, I can see the flaw in that thinking. Well played, Mum and Auntie Chic. Well played.

"Auntie, what is the deal with this washing machine? I put it to 1 and now it's on 5. It's happened three times so far."

My aunt burst out laughing. We laughed together a lot, but somehow this felt very one-sided. "Sweetheart, it goes through a cycle and always ends at 5. You have washed the clothes three times now."

We both laughed. I wish this story ended there, but it didn't. In fact, it was the butt of many jokes for many years. I was known as the book-smart one, not the street-smart one.

The first time I called the Yellow Pages (aging myself here; but there was no Google in the nineties. We had a paper book and number you called to find out phone numbers—true story, youngsters), when I called, they asked me for the name, and I said, "Melissa Gray."

They said, "No, the name of the business you're looking for." Again—butt of joke. So many years that one lasted.

Granny Bel did everything right in my wee-biased Scottish eyes, but when I became a wife and parent, I asked if she could give me one piece of advice, what would it be. And she said, "Start as you mean to go on, with your husband and your kids."

Then enters Eve Rodisky, via Reese Witherspoon's Book Club. I have loved Reese since the days of *Legally Blonde*. She is, after all, the primary reason I became a lawyer and sent my résumé on light-pink, scented paper. So, if she is suggesting it, I am all freaking in.

My hope is this book changes your life forever and creates action-orientated change. Well, that's what Eve Rodisky did for our family. Eve is the author of *Fair Play* and star of the documentary, *Fair Play*, streaming on Hulu. Stop what you are doing right now, and go watch it. Then, order the book and the cards to match it. This is not a sponsored ad. I do not have a discount code, although I should, since I recommend it to everyone. If you are in a relationship, have kids or don't, it's a game-changing book.

Eve came to me on one of those sleepless nights. You know the ones, the ones where you lie awake, wondering if you're screwing up your relationship and your kids and also wondering why batteries only come in As and not Bs. That night, I searched for ways to reset your family and your marriage. We have never been the same since.

Like all things, it starts with us. I know, I know. It sucks. I've looked for easier, softer ways, lassies and lads, but there are none. So, here we are realizing we are, yet again, the problem. Yes, Taylor Swift, we got it.

My work with clients always begins with values. So that Christmas, while at The Magical Lakehouse with the kids, I sat down with each of them, one-on-one, like they were my client, and together we came up with our own set of family values. Everyone agreed "Team" was one of them. We talked about what it meant to be a team.

At this point, my husband and I had really worked through sharing some chores. I hate the dishwasher, so hubby took that. I love laundry—hello, have you smelled Buff City Soap? Best laundry detergent ever, and smells are my love language. So, laundry is mine.

Hubby is a better cook, so he takes on the bulk of cooking, when he isn't traveling for work, although sometimes he spoils us and leaves a delicious surprise for me to bake in the oven for twenty, before he leaves. Hubby handles paying family house bills, and I take care of tutors and sitters and sports. As I'm writing this, he'd just gotten back from school shoe-shopping, and tomorrow I will get the new uniforms. #Team

Michael and I knew we needed to lead our family by example, and, as parents of three sons, we wanted the boys, who would someday be men, to be the fathers who show up, cook, clean, and shoe shop for school. So, it was our job to model it. For our daughter, we wanted her to receive a message that it wasn't up to women to do it all. We wanted to heed Granny Bel's advice and implement the tools from *Fair Play*, with our own twist of values and intentional living.

Along this journey, I realized my relationship with my kids and husband was only as good as the relationship I have with myself. My silent arguments in my head and slow-growing resentments, as I slammed dishes into the dishwasher and picked up the seventeenth paper plate, weren't helping anyone, and they weren't creating a deeper connection with my people. It was time to take this box off the metaphorical shelf and dive deep into it. It was time for those silent arguments in my head to have a voice, and if I couldn't figure this out, my marriage and my family weren't going to make it.

I was drowning. Drowning in the "must be nice." You know what I am talking about—the "must be nice" we silently say as our partner sits down and turns on sports, and we look around the house and wonder 1. How in the *heck* can he relax in said house and 2. *Really? REALLY?*

Of course, I said nothing and went about banging dishes in the dishwasher, falling into my bed at the same time as my eleven-year-old.

The mental load, the second shift, the invisible work and emotional wellbeing of everyone on my shoulders led me to say these words...

"I think we should divorce."

Until this book, I saw no other way out. My company. The kids. My sobriety. My marriage. It became too much. I felt like I was drowning, suffocating, and dying, and those words aren't for dramatic effect.

While I want to blame society for much of this, I also created my own self-imposed prisons. I wasn't being responsible for myself, because if I had been, I would have spoken up sooner. I was a full-time company owner and a full-time mum, you know, A Mum And...

How does this help not raise spoiled brats? Well, the kids got to see us as a team. They were then invited to join that team.

Daily chores, family meetings, Sunday sit-down at the dinner table, card games, helping with the groceries—that is now the norm for them. Toasting bread and buttering it and helping with their lunches. Taking the trash out and feeding the dog, as well as making their beds is now the norm for them. These changes took time. We didn't change everything at once. But it began with identifying our family values and defining what family means.

If your hope is not to raise spoiled, entitled brats who become those adults—yes, those ones, we all know them— then it's time for a *reset*.

I stayed in the pattern too long, because I was asking all the wrong questions. I stayed stuck because I focused on how things were, instead of how they could be.

When you start thinking how it could be, everything changes. Imagine a life where kids make their bed and take out the trash and feed the dog without being asked. Imagine the sense of pride and responsibility you provide by giving them that. Imagine the adult, husband, wife, partner they will become, when family and teamwork become a core value in their ONE.Life.

Sure, it's easier sometimes to do these things yourself, and it can feel like too much work to model instead of martyr. But what if you're depriving your littles of this internal knowing that they can do things, be a part of things, and are an important player on this team? The knowing that this team requires their participation and the rewards are internal?

> **Model instead of martyr.**

As I write this, my family has completely transformed in the last year. My marriage has transformed in the last year, and almost daily my husband and I text each other, saying, *We are the luckiest.*

I had to Thought-Reset the idea that this is just how things are. This is just the dynamic of my family and my marriage. I was wrong. A year later, I am pretty confident there are zero spoiled brats living in our house. I am also confident my marriage has never felt more like a team or more connected than it is today.

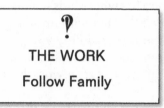

THE WORK

Follow Family

"Family is not an important thing, it's everything."
—Michael J. Fox

o What are your family's values?

Be sure to place them somewhere in the home everyone can see.

o Set a date for you and your partner to go over the division of labor in your home. Be sure to set a few hours, and let it be flexible at first.

o Set a weekly family meeting time and day - Sunday 6pm is good for us. Discuss the upcoming week together. Ask what everyone has going on and who needs extra help this week.

o Set a time weekly with your partner to discuss the week. We like walk and talks, where we discuss how we can help each other, our current workload, and any travel.

o Divide chores up between kids that are age-appropriate. You would be so surprised if you Google *age-appropriate chores*. Our kids are so much more capable than we allow them to be. Our kids set a timer for thirty minutes and like to tackle their chores together. If this doesn't work, assign them individually.

o   We will discuss with kids on (date and time)

Remember: slow and steady wins the race. Changes take time. Implement one at a time until you feel confident to move on to the next one.

CHAPTER 15

UnFollow Divorce

*"And so rock-bottom became the solid foundation
on which I rebuilt my life."*

—J.K. Rowling

What if:
Instead of greener pastures...
Instead of blame...
Instead of fixing...
Instead of repairing...
We *Rebuilt.*
We instead chose, *intentionally*, to rebuild?
I recently sold my minivan. Her name was Betty. I drove Betty for a decade, lassies and lads. A decade. Ten whole years. Betty was my mobile office when my littles were screaming inside the house. I took client calls from inside her. Some people cry on their pillows and in their showers. I cried in Betty. 130,000 miles and years of Cheerios and Goldfish snacks later, she was done.

On one of the occasions Betty decided to stop working was while I was on a trip to The Magical Lakehouse with seven kids and me. You might be wondering what lunatic takes seven kids ten hours away from home, solo—Hi? Nice to meet you.

It was the end of the school year, and the kids wanted to take their friends to their happy place. I agreed on five days, then back to their parents they must go. Six boys aged eleven and under, and my sweet girl Charlie, age five going on fifteen.

I gave these kids the time of their lives—no vacation would ever compare for them.

But it was 4 a.m., and I had to get them home, because it was my fourteenth sobriety birthday, and I was taking a bunch of my clients to see my favorite Irish legend, Dermot Kennedy. When I got everyone inside Betty, they were still all half asleep—it was 4 a.m., after all. I turned the key, full of excitement for the epic adventure we'd had and the joy of what awaited me, time with some of my favorite people and Dermot. The ten-hour drive didn't scare me. I was pumped.

Betty had different plans. She apparently didn't want to leave The Magical Lakehouse. I could hear my husband in my mind: "You really need to sell Betty." But the truth is, I didn't want to sell Betty. Betty was familiar, Betty was comfortable, she was known to me. I knew how she worked (most of the time), and she knew how I worked. I could be myself with Betty. I didn't take care of Betty like I once did, because I was comfortable with her.

When I first got Betty, I really took care of her. She was my everything. Weekly, I would clean her and make sure she was cracker-free for the coming week. I would buy beautiful, scented air fresheners, and diffuse my oils inside her. She drove me back and forth to the hospital with my cancer-warrior son for years. She saw vomit and poop and kids screaming.

Over the years, she started to get worn. The steering wheel was all wrinkled from the sun. I had long stopped putting her in the safety of my garage, often saying, "Who would steal Betty?" She was ripped on either side of the door, and you could see the foam underneath her. A few dings here and there plus a wing mirror that once fell off, and I stopped fixing her up, repairing her, and trying to get her to be what she was before. The truth is, after years of fixing her up, I just stopped taking care of her. I stopped the weekly washes and parking her in the garage away from the Florida heat. I stopped cleaning up the crackers.

The state of my minivan is the state of many of our lives, relationships, marriages, and partnerships.

- We fix.
- We repair.
- We patch up.
- Then, we stop.

But what if we are doing it all wrong?

What if what is really needed is a new version of your relationship?

What if the "you used to do," and "we used to do," and "this never bothered you before," was no longer part of our vicious cycle of communication?

What if, instead, we started fresh? We renew what was, we make new rules, new goals, new shared values, and instead, choose togetherness?

What if we choose to understand our differences?

Know our deal-breakers.

Decide to grow together.

"The number one reason couples divorce is one outgrows the other. It's sad and an atrocity and not necessary," our therapist proclaimed.

It was Friday. *Ugh*, why? I knew better, I told myself. I review my calendars on Sundays, but the night before each new day, I always write a Post-it note of the main things of the next day. Why, oh why?

I'd seen the two-hour appointment with our couple's therapist, Dr. Deborah Brown. I love her. I love him (my husband, Michael), but therapy? Let's just say, I am thankful for Miss Mary, my mentor, who taught me I do not need to like doing things—but I do need to do the things. So, there I was, doing the thing on a Friday 3-5 p.m. The truth is, if I didn't make time for my marriage, I would be making time for my divorce.

Therapy is not new for Michael and me. We have always said it's our insurance policy to no divorce.

But, two decades into our relationship, I was convinced it didn't work. What had been a gorgeous love affair with incredible sex and seeing the world together, all while laughing and eating our way across Europe, just wasn't working. I used our differences against us.

The truth is I knew better.

The truth is I was an anxious, avoidant empath.

The truth is I chose comfort over discomfort.

The truth is I didn't do the work required to take care of us—just like Betty.

Like Betty, I tried hard to repair, fix, and make it like it was before, but the stains weren't coming out, and the parts that were good before now weren't. We no longer shined like we once did. The powerhouse couple who beat stage 4 cancer together with their son, raised a blended family, adopted a child, raised millions for kids' cancer research, stood before thousands of people together on stage—they were no longer seeing each other's highlights and instead, conversations revolved around everything each one of us wanted deleted from the other person.

Date-night repair.

Vacation repair.

Sex repair.

Affection repair.

Compliment repair.

None of it was working. I met Michael when I was twenty, and now, at forty, I was not the same. He was not the same. We were not the same, and yet I pined for what was.

We were not fixing and repairing any longer—that didn't work. So, we had to ask different questions. Instead of asking questions on how to get back to what we had, we asked questions like, what kind of marriage do we want now? Today? What is exciting about marriage? Where can we find joy in each other?

We began rebuilding. We began focusing on:

- Communication
- Shared priorities
- Connection
- Trust

"In that order," Dr. Brown said gently that Friday afternoon. She went on to tell us that communication was about emotional self-regulation, that it was our job to create safe spaces for each other to communicate. That this was the key to a healthy marriage.

Michael and I are both trained lawyers. Michael is one of the most successful trial attorneys in the U.S., losing only one case in thirty years. He argues for a living. I am an anxious avoidant, with a yelly Scottish voice. Together, we were learning the "be right or be happy" rule.

The truth is, we both grew in different ways; but trauma and drama created a wedge. Most families who have children with cancer divorce. We have witnessed many, and it's heartbreaking. But I wonder if trying to fix or repair a marriage back to the way it was, is part of the issue. The truth is, for most couples in long-term relationships, we fall into this trap, believing that you can get back to where the marriage was, instead of looking for true gold that can be found in taking down the house and rebuilding a whole new one. A rebuild that would change your ONE.Life and create ripples throughout your family.

> *A rebuild that would change your ONE.Life and create ripples throughout your family.*

So, we *choose to build* a new relationship.
One not based on the past.
One focused on our future.

We needed to ask different questions. Questions that excited us about our future and were not focused on our past. Not focused on our mutual lacking, but instead on our mutual winnings.

We opted to keep our communication at conversation level, not like the cross-examination at a trial.

We opted to end conversations when they were emotionally charged and logic had been outrun by emotions.

We opted to individually handle our own past traumas, knowing that they were informing some of our current reactive patterns.

We opted to honestly communicate about the power dynamic in our relationship, knowing, if we didn't, resentment would kill our new relationship we were building.

We opted to create new rules, new boundaries—no longer was punishing behavior allowed, like stonewalling, walking away, changing plans, ignoring plans, or passive-aggressive behavior.

We opted for timeouts, with agreed upon times on when to come back to the issue. We opted to know each other's buttons and to be intentional about not pushing them, knowing otherwise this would steal the security and safety we were building in each other.

We opted to get to know our reactive behavior patterns and decide new ways to react and then help each other stay accountable to that.

We opted to no longer stay silent, knowing we both needed to use our voices in this new relationship we were building with each other.

While I'm just a lawyer who is master-certified in professional life coaching, my biggest asset to my clients in relationships is I have been in a relationship for twenty years, with a decade of couple's therapy under my belt. That requires courage, resilience, forgiveness, connection, communication, and work. Serious work. The odd car wash and quick blow out of the crackers doesn't cut it.

Your rock-bottom becomes the foundation of your rebuild.

This book is about questioning everything. Literally every single thing. But doing it in a way that excites you about the work, not terrifies you. It's about *really* doing the work. It's about creating a pathway to an EMPOWERED.Life. Perhaps you will read this chapter, do the work, and feel that divorce is the right path for you. It is for many. But then there are the others who simply need to learn new skills to create the relationship they desire. I know, for myself and many of my clients, I've witnessed what this work does and how it can change the trajectory of your ONE.Life.

I know this was true for my clients, Shannon and Dan.

While we have subconsciously been trained on how to fall in love—cue every movie ever made—we have little guidance on how to maintain a relationship.

I met Shannon first.

"Hey, you don't know me, but I know you, and I have been looking for a life coach."

From the moment I saw Shannon, I fell for her. You know, in that way where someone's energy is just electric and beautiful and loud. As someone who no longer takes offense (it took some work) to the loud comment, we were instantly complementing each other left and right. Shannon is joy, yet something was off.

When I meet new clients, I get excited for them. I know they are nervous, and I desire to make them comfortable, but at the same time, I know they are serious when they contact me. They are ready to do the work.

Shannon partakes in the Busy Olympics. She has four young children and multiple companies, plus she is often chairing a local gala and, well, never stops. Often, stopping is painful for lassies like Shannon—it means staring directly right into the eyes of something we fear. I work with many lassies who partake in the Busy Olympics. They are my favorites. Why? I was one, and I know the joy that lives on the other side of this particular work.

If you are close enough to a woman who volunteers for everything, raises kids, runs the local gala, and bakes all the cakes for the bake sale, do me a favor. Lovingly shake her. Okay, maybe don't physically shake her, but could you buy her this book and earmark this chapter? Too obvious?

The struggle is, lassies and lads, if everything is important, nothing is important.

This is why every client I work with begins with value work and figuring out what is truly a priority in their life.

Many of our marriages and relationships are dying at the hands of the Busy Olympics.

Yet, we look around and see everyone is doing... everything. Or so we believe.

If you take away one thing from this book, take this: *UnFollow* everyone who seems to or appears to act like:

1. They have it all together.
2. Does it *all*.

It's false advertising, and it's killing us. Literally.

"Shannon, how can I help you?"

"Well, I have it all. I have four amazing sons and an incredible husband, but I am scared my kids are going to end up spoiled. And, well, Dan and I... Dan and I..." She struggled to get the words out, which, considering the fluidity of our conversation to date, was surprising.

"I want to do things and go places and travel, and he doesn't. I want to grow with him. I love him, but I just don't know if we can." There was a sadness to her voice. Shannon and Dan had been together for sixteen years. "I feel like our family needs something... I don't know what. I just feel like I am failing somehow."

Shannon is not alone. Many of us lassies wonder daily, usually in the wee hours of the morning, are we doing enough? Am I screwing up my kids? Will my marriage weather this particular storm?

About six months into working with Shannon, she invited me to spend time with her family. Anytime a family invites me into their home, it's truly an honor. Shannon and Dan invited me over to spend time with them and their four sons. I watched them fish and the chaos that is four kids. I live this life, and I am comfortable here.

I sat at the dinner table and played a card game that allowed me to get to know each of the four kids and the dynamic of Dan and Shannon. Shannon had alluded to Dan needing me as his coach, but I knew I couldn't help this family unless I saw them in their home and environment.

At the end of the visit, Shannon and Dan and the kids walked me to the car, and they all waved me off. It was a beautiful ending to a fun bonding night for them as a family. The next day, Shannon called me.

"Well...? Do you see and feel what I feel? Can I give Dan your number?"

Dan called me the next day, and therein began a year of coaching him. We would meet for two hours at a time. Dan was becoming self-aware, seeing his role in the family, and discovering ways he wanted to rebuild his marriage with Shannon.

In between individual sessions, I met with them as a couple. Shannon was saying things she never had said before, and so was Dan. This was because, with a third party, we tend to feel safer than on our own. After years of avoiding some of these hard conversations, Shannon and Dan decided to rebuild. To stop patching up and repairing, and instead to rebuild. To start over. A clean slate. A new kind of marriage. For them and for their children.

Most of us don't envy the relationships of our parents. Many of us are adult children of divorce. Many of us are undoing much of what we witnessed growing up, and we desire and seek something different. Yet, how then do we have what we desire? Knowing what we desire is part one. Part two is obtaining it. That's the work of this chapter, lassies and lads. That's the work Shannon and Dan did.

While I understand no relationship—yes, *no* relationship, at least not one with two self-aware people—can be all sunshine and rainbows, a relationship is about sharing the umbrella. It's about a team.

The Gottman institute is the GOAT in research into relationships. They have followed thousands of couples over decades, even having a house where they watched couples and how they communicate. That research has given the Institute ninety-percent accuracy in predicting divorce in couples. Half of all marriages that end do so in the first seven years. This wasn't what Shannon and Dan wanted. They wanted tools. They wanted and needed to do the work.

If love is a verb and not something you give someone or receive from them, then what is love? After working closely with couples like Shannon and Dan and their family, plus my own relationship experience, I believe that a bond with another person is only as strong as the bond you have with yourself. This is why couples work requires intensive solo work as well, to be the most effective.

- I can only love you… if I love me.
- I can only love you… as well as I love me.
- I can only love you… as deeply as I love me.
- I can only grow with you… if I grow with me
- I can only connect with you… if I can connect with me
- I can only love you… if I love me.

This is why the relationship with self is the biggest ROI of all the work we do in life. The ripple effect of this work impacts every single area of our life. Dan needed to do the work, and while Shannon and he still thank me for changing their lives, the truth is *they* changed their lives. They did the work, no one else. I was merely a facilitator.

Lassies and lads, no one, I repeat, *no one* person can be the sole source of your happiness. *You* are the source of your happiness, and doing that work will bring more joy and connection in every relationship in your ONE.Life. Understanding this can rebuild marriages and relationships.

**It's time to stop saving marriages
and instead begin rebuilding them.**

What if you stop looking for your person to check all the boxes and instead look to edit the story together, knowing there will be a need for highlighting and deleting often?

I have a sign in my house that says, *Highlight and Delete*. It means a lot to me. I have a lot of signs around my house, because I believe in training my subconscious with constant reminders of how I want this one ONE.Life to go. In relationships, we need a lot more grace than we give.

> *"The problem in unhappy relationships is not
> that people need to be more positive.
> It's that they need to notice the positive that's already there."*
> —John and Julie Gottman

Jean and Charlie King epitomize that quote. My grandparents were married sixty-five years, and while I believe in quality over quantity, they are my only example of both. My Gran and Papa raised six kids, and they buried one child. Three of their kids buried their babies, and my gran battled and beat cancer.

Growing up, I would have dinner with them, and they would say, "Okay, time for our walk, Melissa."

Every night after dinner, they held hands and walked the neighborhood. My grandfather hated shopping, yet he sat outside stores with my gran for hours. My gran couldn't stand football, yet she sat aside my grandfather to watch it.

"Ohhhhh, *Charlieeeeee*," she would say in her sweet Scottish accent, the most endearing voice you ever heard.

While they were visiting my husband and me in the States, we were all watching a movie.

Gran, tired, said, "I am going to my bed, I am tired." And as she walked upstairs slowly, she said, "*Charliiiiieeee*, I said I am going to maa bed."

Papa, who was glaring intently at the TV, loving our movie, said, "Oh well, I am quite tired. Better be getting to my bed."

My husband and I giggled together and have laughed at that moment a million times.

I often ask myself, is this compromise or self-sacrifice, when I am confronted with issues inside my marriage. I think I've gotten this wrong many times. I think I've misinterpreted compromise for control. But watching my grandparents as role models shifted that in me.

A question to ask yourself is this: is this self-sacrifice or compromise?

My Gran and Papa mastered this. And they mastered it in spite of circumstances. When our son was diagnosed with cancer and life as we knew it changed forever, Michael and I both said, "Let's not save our son and then raise him in two homes." And yet, we came scarily close to doing just that.

When Gran passed away a year ago, it shook our family to the core, but she had all her living children and grandchildren and, of course, her one true love right beside her. I often think of her when I think how I want to make my eighty-year-old

?

self proud. My gran didn't need to give me words of wisdom for marriage. She lived her wisdom.

If we don't make time for our marriage, we will be making time for our divorce.

For those of us ready for a rebuild, it's time to start asking the right questions with excitement. Questions that excite you about a future where your marriage is recreated, and you feel like you are a team. A marriage where compromise doesn't feel like sacrifice. A marriage where your values align. A marriage where you learn to love yourself, knowing your marriage will only be enriched by your own personal work. A marriage where we don't avoid work by participating in the Busy Olympics. A marriage where communication is key.

Our questions can keep us stuck or keep us growing. Ask them wisely.

THE WORK

Follow Rebuild

"In marriage, when we honor and celebrate each other, we're freed up to be the best people we can be."
—Dr. John Gottman

Feel free to do this alone or, better yet, ask your partner/spouse to read the chapter with you and decide to rebuild together. Just a suggestion.

o   Is my misery caused solely by this one person? Is this true? Is this helpful?

o   What marriage do I know and admire?

o   A marriage/relationship mentor I could seek is

o   I will contact them (date and time)

o   What does a partnership or marriage mean to you?

o   What fulfills you?

o   I will start using I FEEL statements instead of YOU make me feel when communicating. For example, in my relationship, I:

o   I am highlighting these three things about my partner/spouse.

o   Today I will share one of them with her/him.

o   One thing I know I need to apologize for with my partner is:

o   I will apologize (date time).

o   I am committed to learning ways to self-soothe, instead of using unhealthy patterns. One thing I plan to do when I am upset is:

o   I know emotional regulation is vital for a healthy relationship. One way I plan to work on this is:

o   When communicating with my partner/spouse, I will keep things at conversation level, and when I feel like I am getting off the beam with this, I will instantly:

o   I will not have conversations when I am emotionally charged and logic outruns my emotions. Other rules my partner/spouse and I have decided to have are:

o   I know I cannot do this alone, and as a result, my partner and I are seeking a coach/therapist/ mentor. I am committing to do this by (date and time).

o   I have opted to have timeouts in our relationship but always agreeing to a date and time to come back to the conversation. Other ways I can ensure healthy communications are:

o   I know that punishing behavior is extremely damaging in our relationship. Ways I have done this in the past include:

o   We are choosing to use our voices and not avoid our relationship issues. One issue I would really like to address is:

o   I plan to address it (date and time).

o   My partner's buttons include:

I will actively and intentionally not push these buttons, knowing that love is a verb and I am here to rebuild.

o I know stonewalling (ignoring) is a silent relationship-killer, and I am here to rebuild. My partner has permission to keep me accountable, should I fall into old patterns. I plan to communicate this to him/her by/on (date and time).

CHAPTER 16

UnFollow Work-Life Balance

"Work-life alignment is not hours in the day; it's energy allocated to the right things."
—Matthew Kelly

What is the best day of your life? No, really. Not the answer you *think* you should write here. No one needs to know—just you and me.

You don't have to tell me it was the birth of your kid; you already know that's not mine. You don't have to say it's the day you got married—no judgment if it is; I just know you're lying. I've yet to meet anyone who said it was the best day of their life. All that stress about who sits where and will everyone have a good time.

So, you ready to be honest? How about I go first? Then, write me and tell me yours. Deal? If this scares you, don't worry, I am going to give some ways to determine the day. Why is this important, you ask? And why, oh why, must it be only one day? I couldn't possibly...

Today. It's today. Today, I get to do something I've been trying to do for ten years. I feel nervous butterflies like the night before Christmas Day as a kid, the feeling I get before being on stage to keynote or hosting a workshop or a retreat. The feeling I get before doing something I have never done before. The unknown, the challenge of it. This feels like the day of my first marathon. The first time I went category 4 whitewater rafting. The first time I saw The Magical

Lakehouse. The best days of our life tend to be the first time we have done something. For ten years, I've attempted over and over to do this, and every time, I was rejected. In fact, so was one of my besties, Kay Rawlins, the founder of Orlando City Soccer Club (in Orlando, Kay is literally the queen of our city, and she was also rejected over and over, just like me).

A text popped up on my phone.

> Kay: *Melissa, I know you have been waiting a decade to do this, and the time has come. Let's blow this up. Let's get media involved and publicize this across the U.S.*

My teeth clenched, I choked up, water filled my hazel-brown eyes. I pressed my lips together and wiped my eyes to re-read the text message again. I've been disappointed before.

> *Are you serious?* I quickly respond.
> *So serious. Let's get a date on the calendar.*

A few weeks after that text, Kay and I got to fulfill a promise we made to each other, and to all the kids impacted by pediatric cancer.

Kay and I, my three sons, their bestie Carter, and Sam, my teammate in my companies for the last seven years, all arrived together. It was time.

Pat, who was directing the show that day, wanted to shoot a video of us entering and interview all my kids about what today meant for their mum and for them. Then, they wanted to interview Kay and me. We both cried.

We both love each other so much and have been through some very hard times together. Kay's husband openly cheated on her, and she went through a very public divorce. Kay then helped me start my nonprofit, as she has her own, and has

?

become a huge advocate for kids' cancer, while serving on my board since its inception.

I picked up the clipboard, filled in the questions, and they took my blood pressure and temperature.

The time was here. Today, we get to donate blood for the first time.

"Okay, girls, sit up on the chairs. We will do this together."

As the nurse began tapping on my veins, *boom!* First try, and it was in. I watched my son have many needles in him, and at the end of treatment, his veins were so bad that, one time, I counted twelve attempts it took the nurse to get a vein. Meanwhile, I was holding him down as he was screaming. I flashed back to this memory and was reminded of why today was the best day of my ONE.Life.

Then it began. The blood started filling in the small bag hanging beside me, and just like that, Kay and I looked at each other, sharing yet another incredible memory.

That day, we became blood donors.

Pat, the head of PR for One Blood, interviewed me while my blood is being drawn. "Why is today so important to you? You said it's the best day of your life."

"It is," I responded. "Nothing so far has beaten this, and I am thirty-nine years old. My son, Cannon, is alive because of blood and platelet donors. I would take him to our local hospital, and he would be lifeless, white, pale, with no energy, and could barely hold his head up. I can still see that image in my head. It haunts me. Then, he would receive red blood cells and platelets, and within a few hours, that very same lifeless two-year-old was chasing his amazing nurses and doctors around the floor. Seeing the impact of donations up close forever changed my perspective on blood donations. And now, today, I get to be a part of the solution."

Lassies and lads, I do not say this for dramatic effect but as truth. My truth. I have been to more kids' funerals than adults' funerals. Being at a one-year-old's, a five-year-old's, an eight-year-old's, an eleven-year- old's funeral changes a person.

Seeing the tiny wooden box, not bigger than the length of a car door, being pushed up a church aisle as your cancer-mum friend sobs over her child is why.

Cannon is alive, but most of his friends are not. So, while our foundation impacts hundreds of kids' lives every single day, for me it's not enough. I can never, ever repay what was given to Cannon, but my job is to try during this ONE.Life. *Today* is the best day of my life because this is in alignment with every single value I possess as a woman and mum.

I don't believe in work-life balance, because, as much as I am the half-full-girl type of lassie, my husband has rubbed off on me, and I am also a realist. My realist side has accepted that balance is a crock of horse dung.

Let's stop using energy for work-life balance and instead let's move toward work-life alignment. When we focus on balance, we are constantly disappointed or living in guilt. Guilt when with our families, guilt when we are at work. Focusing on alignment allows our energy to be directed in deliberate and intentional ways minus the guilt.

> *"Don't balance work and life; integrate them"*
> —Arianna Huffington

Let's agree to stop using our energy on work-life balance and instead choose work-life alignment.

What does alignment mean? Don't Google it; you will spend hours with no real answer at the end. This is what my clients and I think it means. Feel free to use whatever definition works for you.

Alignment is when your values are in play with your actions.

My clients, and also my kids and I, journal every day. In my coaching programs, I created a journal that focuses on morning intentions and nightly reflections.

In our morning intentions, we ask ourselves: what value is most in play today? In our nightly reflections, we ask ourselves: how was my value game today, on a scale of 1 to 10?

Questioning everything with excitement is about using the data to better your ONE.Life; knowing that, by answering the questions, the data allows you to get to a place where you can even have the best day of your life.

When I donated blood, it hit all my values.

- Connection: with one of my besties, Kay.
- Growth: I had never done it before.
- Leadership: I got to be a part of letting the world know that British people can now donate in the U.S., thanks to a change by the federal government.
- Gratitude: this is my way of having thanks for every ounce of blood and life-saving platelets my son received.
- Family: my three sons were with me, and nothing makes my heart happier than when my kids partake in my keynote speeches or my workshops or anything I do. They love being a part of my work, and I am happiest when they are in the crowd. I call it, "Bring your kid to work day" on my social media.
- Health: in order to donate blood, you must be healthy; health is very important to me.

So, all six of my values were in place that day.

When I work with clients, we look deeply into their values. I typically say, "Show me your calendar, and I will tell you your core values."

Usually, we spend a solid month looking at their values, proving and testing each one of them. Many of us think something is of value to us, but actually, it's typically valuable to someone else, so we think it should be ours.

One of my mum clients didn't have family as a value, and she felt horrible, beating herself up about it. We can never have the best days of our lives if we live other people's values. This client, after a year of work, not only accepted this wasn't her value, but she realized something that was better for her: *peace*. And that's how she loves her people, by creating peace for them, by being the peace in her home.

Personally, when I began this work on values over five years ago, I didn't want to put *leadership* down. Maybe it was false humility, or maybe it was all those years of being called bossy that had me pushing away from my natural-born leadership skills. The truth is, I came out of the womb this way—just ask my mum how I used to parent my siblings.

It's funny, now that I am raising a girl myself, my daughter, Charlie. Karma, you got me, and my mum now laughs at the stories I tell her. The truth is, leadership is important to me. I associate it with being a part of the solution, changing the status quo, and pushing my learnings into the lassies and lads who ask me to.

The time is now to *UnFollow* work-life balance, the story we have been served by society—again, in my humble opinion. The time is now to seek and *Follow* alignment with our ONE.Life and work. More and more homes are now dual-income homes, meaning the time is now to really get into this deep work.

I've worked with lassies and lads, especially high-performance people, who felt stuck and unfulfilled. When we did this work, they moved from seeking the work-life balance to work-life alignment.

The days of guilt at work and guilt at home need to *go*. It's a vicious game, and none of us are winning it.

Brian is a very accomplished client and friend. Wicked smart, innovative, forward-thinking, and has a great personality to match.

I met Brian when I was consulting with him about my company. One of his companies builds some of the most creative and innovative brands. I wanted to discuss my brand and what he could do for my companies.

❦

Brian was so impressed with my company presentation and what I was attempting to do with my work that he ended up hiring me as his coach. That makes us both laugh.

Brian's brain had made some incredible plays with major brands, and his entrepreneurial spirit was on full go-mode when we met. Brian worked until the wee hours then. As a recovered workaholic, it takes one to know one.

For many high-performance people, work is just so easy for us. It's comfortable and joyful and challenging, and it's easy to be mesmerized by it. As someone who lived the same life as Brian and completely burnt out, I knew what we needed to do. Often, we do not see the wood for the trees, and I believe a good coach shows you what to do. But a *great* coach (still working on my humility, clearly), a great coach doesn't tell you to do anything. They instead show you what you're doing by asking questions that change your ONE.Life.

I asked Brian questions he had never been asked before.

"Tell me about the best day of your life."

Most people are stumped by this question. Typically, I love asking it at the beginning of working with someone and then later again, after we do six months of coaching.

Once Brian knew his values and why some things made him tick and others didn't, it became the anchor of what he said *yes* to and what he said *no* to. It became his way of checking if he was on the beam. It became his way of getting back on the beam. It became the way he lives his ONE.Life.

It's been a year since we did this work together, and recently, we shared a pot of tea. When Brian and I first met, he interrupted our meeting a few times to check his phone and direct his team quickly. This wasn't a time-management issue, a leadership issue, or a delegation issue. Nope. This was a work-life alignment issue.

But this Brian, the one I was meeting a year later...

I told the receptionist in his super-hip office that I was there for him. She said, "Just go on back. You know where he is."

I walked through this office, smiling. The energy felt lighter. I'd noticed recently that even their social media had skits and jokes and felt more fun.

I walked into his office, and he instantly stepped up from behind his desk and gave me a hug. His face, his energy, his tan, his clothes—everything felt different to me.

"Hey, let's go out for a cup of tea. There is a great place around the corner."

I instantly smiled inside. For many, many meetings with Brian, I had always been on a strict window of time with him, knowing he had meetings pending on each side of ours, and margin was not something he ever had. But that day? That day, we were leaving the office and having tea.

We ordered our tea and settled into the corner for a yearly check-in.

"You changed my life."

I love it when clients say this, because instantly, I get to respond, "Wrong! *You* changed your life. You did the work, not me. I just ask really great questions."

We both laughed.

"Seriously."

"You would be so proud of me. I don't work until 2 a.m. anymore, and I have never been more happy or more excited about the future than I am right now. My business has never been better, and next week, my wife and I go alone to Greece. Europe, Melissa! Europe *alone*."

Ever since I allowed tears to come to my eyes in my early thirties, I have had little control over choking up and tears filling my eyes. I have created my own rules in my company, and I cry when my clients' lives change. I get emotional. Imagine a life where your business has never been better, and you make time for this ONE.Life and hit Europe with your wife.

The reason Brian didn't burn out, the reason he doesn't feel torn between work and home life, the reason he is winning in this ONE.Life, is because he chose to *UnFollow* the idea of work-life balance. He stopped using energy for this foolish goal and instead chose to *Follow* work-life alignment.

The ripple effect in Brian's work is that his wife and kids win. They have a present and fun husband and father, who is home for dinner. His team wins with a new, incredible client list that inspires all of them and an office space filled with laughter.

Questioning everything with excitement moves you away from burnout and the foolish notion of balance.

Alignment is *exciting*!

When your values are in play in your actions, you don't work until 2 a.m., because you don't have to get the work done. You take vacations to Europe, because your leadership is on point and your team can operate without you—because that's how you designed it.

As I told Brian many times: ONE.Life—how are you going to live it? No do-overs. No dress rehearsal. This is it.

THE WORK

Follow Work-Life Alignment

o   The best day of my life is:

o   I know this is the best day of my life because:

o   The core values I plan to review in my life are:

o   The evidence I found of these values in my life are:

o   One thing I know could get me off the beam and burn me out is:

o   When I show up at work, I want to show up like:

o   When I show up at home, I want to show up like:

o   I am bringing my energy for these people right now:

o   I define alignment as:

o   For me alignment *looks* like:

o   For me alignment *feels* like:

o   One change I plan to make after reading this chapter is:

CHAPTER 17

UnFollow Blowing out *Her* Candle

"The success of every woman should be the inspiration to another, we should raise each other up."
—Serena Williams

"**O**f *course*, you won, looking like that," she said, as she eyed me up and down.

Some of us need a little refresher on, "If you have nothing kind to say, don't say anything at all." But something my clients and I work on often is keeping our side of the street clean and never comparing our start of the journey to someone's middle or end. It's easily done, but blowing out someone else's candle doesn't make yours shine brighter, lassies and lads.

Blowing out someone else's candle doesn't make yours shine brighter.

When I started our nonprofit, people would ask me about other, larger nonprofits. You know, when people want to hear you tear others down. But it's not my style. And, while envy can be quite natural, it's not a place one should live. When your thoughts, which are just sentences in our mind like, "Of course, you won, looking like that," actually come out of your mouth, it's ugly.

You are what you think, lassies and lads, and if you spend your energy thinking about others, you are not winning in your own life. First comes resentful, then comes bitter, and finally, unkind. We all know them. We don't want to be them. I had just won a large sum of money for our nonprofit for a speaking competition and, honestly, had never worked so hard for anything in my life. The truth is I have been blessed with some amazing genes, lassies and lads. My mum is smoking hot. She is always asked if she is my sister—imagine my joy when people say it. That said, I like to think my eight years of law school and being a lawyer, coupled with my hundreds of hours prepping for this speech for months, are what got me there, not my cute clothes and great genes. I like to imagine that 1,000 voters didn't vote for me because of how I looked.

But if your thought about yourself is that life has treated you unfairly because of how you look, you may then believe that thought. And when we repeat thoughts enough, they become a part of our core beliefs.

Our most repeated thoughts become our beliefs.

So, when you see someone with great genes winning something, your wee noggin thinks, "Well, of course she won."

This is the reason I encourage my clients to regularly Thought-Detox. A thought detox is a concept I came up with to help clients with their thoughts, in the same way a detox helps the body. As a lassie who has done body detoxes for years, the name just stuck.

A thought detox works for your brain the way a detox works for your body.

A thought detox is the act of writing down all your thoughts as a way of helping you live in solutions, not problems. When you review your thought detoxes, you notice patterns in your thinking, and with practice, you find your true beliefs about yourself.

Consider this: when you think of a math problem in your head, the answer is first hard to get to, and if you do get to the answer, it typically takes a lot longer. When you write things down, you get to solutions and get to them faster.

In my country, we say," Dinnae keep it awe in yer heed."

In other words, don't keep all 60,000 thoughts in your head each day.

Do not believe all the thoughts in your wee noggin, lassies and lads.

Thought-Detox and SPEAR

My retreat at The Magical Lakehouse is called Waterfalls and Wonder, and yup, you guessed it, every retreat includes a hike to magical waterfalls. When we reach the summit, each of us takes a turn under the waterfall. The power of the waterfall makes it hard to breathe, hard to focus, and, frankly, it's pretty painful.

This is what it's like if you allow all 60,000 thoughts a day to become your beliefs. Instead, I encourage my clients to stand back. Stand behind the waterfall, watch it, observe it, and see its beauty, its power. It's there we decide what we highlight and what we delete.

When we get in the habit of doing thought detoxes, we get in the habit of observing what our thoughts mean and which ones we want to dig into. But keeping it all in your head is like constantly standing under a waterfall all day, every day—no thanks. So, a thought like, "Why her and not me" or "She only won because of her looks," we can take apart. A thought is merely a sentence in our head.

After my clients thought-detox, I have them use my SPEAR tool. The SPEAR tool I created is a combination of cognitive behavioral therapy and methods my coaches have used on me. And since my superpower is simplicity, I've attempted to take some of the complexities of each of those teachings and create a tool you can use in car line. You're welcome.

Think of a spear; we call it a javelin in my country, a large, pointy tool that you throw. When you allow your unconscious brain to run the show, you don't know what direction that spear is going. But when you do a thought reset, you can decide consciously what direction you would like the spear to go in.

The SPEAR is a symbol for your ONE.Life.

> *"If you think about it long enough it will happen."*
> —Jeanette Winterson

Case in point, I recently got a new car. Oh, lassies, she is fancy. I loved Betty, my minivan, but Fern Forest Wiggins— she is a dream. After a decade of driving a minivan, I can't believe I no longer need to carry around a portable speaker to listen to music. And holy cow, the seat massages me and blows hot or cold air on my arse. What is this new world?

The point is, before I bought this car, my kids and I never saw her fancy model or took note of any car remotely like her. Why? It wasn't important. I hadn't told my brain, and my kids hadn't told their brains, that a black Lincoln Navigator was important. And since our brain can only take in so much information, we are constantly filtering out what we think is unimportant data.

Imagine if every single thing our eyes saw, our brain thought about. Just look at your desk or where you're sitting. Your brain can't possibly take in everything, so what you tell it is important is what it brings to your attention. Hence, why brain training can be a vital shift in our lives.

Guess what car several times a day my kids and I see? *Yep, all* the black Lincoln Navigators. Why? We have told our brains over and over this is important to us, so our brain brings them to our attention. This is why we so often become what we consume. Ever stayed up late, watching a murder show? I

? 175

know, I know—me, too. I have spent way too many nights watching BritBox reruns of *Vera*, only to have dreams about the storyline.

When we begin to make the unconscious conscious, we begin to truly reset our lives. We begin to have control over the direction of our lives. We begin to choose where to throw that metaphorical spear.

THE WORK

Follow Brain Training

"The best project you'll ever work on is you."
—Sonny Franco

We begin by brain training.

It begins with thought-detoxing. It continues with thought-resetting, and it deepens by using SPEAR, a tool for self-coaching.

Let's use the thought the lassie who said to me, "Of course, you won, looking like that." And I will show you, in real time, how this work can truly impact your ONE.Life, lassies and lads. Buckle up. Let's Go!

So, the S in SPEAR stands for *subject matter*. The subject matter here is someone's appearance. In reality, this is just factual; it's neutral, it's easy to find. Other subjects could be marriage, money, relationships. These subjects don't have any emotions or thoughts or beliefs tied to them, until we decide what those thoughts, beliefs, etc., are. So, they are, in fact, neutral, and the meaning of them is truly up to us. Marriage is a neutral subject, but then we humans attach meaning to it. Before that, it is just a subject matter.

P is Perception: Don't look up what this means. Your brain will explode with the research into the topic. I've simplified it to this: "our thoughts become our beliefs, and our beliefs are how we see the world." I often ask my clients what glasses they are wearing—the rosy ones or the dark ones? The choice of glasses impacts how we see the world.

Hypothetically, her thought is that people who look a certain way win things. The belief is usually much deeper and could be, "I am not good enough, because I look different than her." She has attached meaning to the way I look and dress, based on her repeated thoughts, which have become her beliefs and how she sees the world.

E is the *Emotion* behind it. Again, the research on emotions and feelings is vast, and so I simplify this to mean our thoughts are charged by our emotions, often creating feelings in us. So, if she believes she is not good enough and only those types of lassies win, the emotion behind it could be sadness, which, if we go deeper, could be loneliness, or even jealousy.

A is for Action: the action was saying some words that could appear unkind.

R is Result: she likely left the event not feeling that great and wondering why.

If we thought-detox this, we can then decide how we wish to thought-reset. This is making the unconscious conscious. True magic can happen here.

This would be like writing stream-of-consciousness thoughts for pages and pages and seeing what comes up. The thought reset would be, then, on purpose, intentionally choosing how you seek to think about something.

Subject stays the same: appearance.

Perception: I imagine one would like to think that good genes are not required to succeed in life. I would coach my client to even search for lots of people who look different from the winner and note all the accomplishments they have. Perhaps a shift here could be that *talent* and *hard work* are factors in winning.

Thought: She won on her merit. People win on their merit.

Belief: Women of all shapes, sizes, and race can be successful.

Emotion: The emotion completely shifts. It's feelings of hope and joy and maybe even feeling happy for the lass. Too far?

Action: Her action could have looked like genuinely congratulating the lass, knowing this could be her, too.

Results: leave the event feeling good and truly enjoying the time there.

Okay, okay, you can stop the eye-rolling. But this tool is like a muscle: you have to work it to see it. It takes constant practice, but after six months of practicing in my intensive coaching program, lassies and lads have found new ways of never needing to blow out other people's candles, among many other things. They can spot their thoughts, they detox them, they reset them, and then they decide which result they want and they practice that.

In early sobriety, I recall asking a lad who had two years sobriety why he kept going to recovery meetings. At less than thirty days sober, I couldn't even imagine being sober two years.

He tapped his head and said, "Peace of mind, lass. Peace of mind."

Imagine a life where your thoughts don't bully you.

A life where you had tools to help move into peace of mind.

I aspire to have this, and so do my clients. It takes work. But if you work it, it's worth it.

If you work it, it's worth it.

Visit melissawiggins.life/UnFollow to complete your very first brain-training session. You can decide where you want the SPEAR to go. If you do this exercise, be sure to share and tag me on social. You really would make a wee Scottish lassie so frickin' happy.

Remember to tackle this work with excitement. Focus on the peace of mind that can happen when your thoughts don't bully you. When you can intentionally and on purpose choose the direction that you seek your ONE.Life to go.

The SPEAR is yours. All you have to do is pick it up.

CHAPTER 18

UnFollow Words

"Don't talk about it, be about it."

—Unknown

Energy is the most raw, real, honest version of communication. I can feel you before I hear you.

As part of the research for this book, my publisher suggested I ask people close to me to say the words they associate with me. I've asked my clients to do this in the past, as well as to write their own obituary, so I wasn't fazed by this exercise.

"You are not what you think you are. You are not what other people think you are. You are what you think other people think you are."

—Anonymous

With that quote in mind, I asked my mum and sister.

My mum responded with some few delightful words— hello, mum duty. But in the mix was a word that makes hairs go up the back of my neck.

Sensitive.

Did the hairs on your body just stand up?

You see, I was raised in Scotland, and I didn't cry until I was in my thirties, all for the greater good of not being seen or called *sensitive.*

❡ 181

I was raised to "Get on with it" and "Water off a duck's back."

So, I pretended, and then I used alcohol to numb.

As I sit here, fourteen years sober, I can proudly say I am sensitive, but not in the way one might imagine. I love a joke and really do accept life on life's terms. But I am sensitive to other people—I am intuitive. I can feel you before I hear you.

I can walk into any room, whether I know the people or not, and I can sense their anxiety, their joy. Around people I know, I can tell in a few short seconds whether something is okay or not. My hypervigilance has pushed me deeper into the work of my energy and how I am showing up and choosing the friends, colleagues, and family members I seek to be around.

My clients and I focus a lot on energy and the different kinds of energy.

The Physical Kind

Imagine, every morning you wake up, you have a Mason jar filled with water beside your bed. It's filled to the brim when you wake up, but as soon as your eyes open, the water level goes down with each decision, interaction, and activity you do. The checking social media, the talking to your mum, the client work, the getting four kids out the door by 7:15 a.m. (just me?), all of it. This jar allows you to decide each day where you need to focus and whether you can take the call now or do it tomorrow.

Transition Energy (or, as I like to call it, Minivan Moments)

The energy where I close my eyes and decide how I need to show up for the next part of my day and life. Today, my last client call finished at 2:30 p.m. This gave me a short thirty-minute window before I picked up the four bairns.

So, I took a moment. I closed my eyes. I thought about what my kids needed from me for the next hour and how I could give them that. I thought about the intention word, the one I wrote in my morning journal, for how I wanted to show up— usually, it's *fun*. Being a fun mum is tattooed on my heart.

Being the owner of my energy means I need to consider facts that can knock me off the beam. I know, if I am to be a fun mum from 3-4 p.m., before I head back to work mode, something that always gets me off the beam is my phone. It could be a quick client text to reschedule their one-on-one that I need to respond to, and that now has my head thinking about my calendar and how best to respond. It could be a text about a child newly diagnosed with cancer. It could be great news, which also sends me in a different direction.

Being the boss of my energy means I have to come up with solutions. I bought a kSafe, which is a lock-lid safe with a timer that stores devices for whatever period of time you choose. My phone is locked in there for an hour, and I cannot retrieve it, even if I want to. Some of you might have killer restraint and not need this, but for those of you who, like me, might need a little help, it's a great solution. Actually, without the kSafe, this book would not be in your hands. It's helped me focus on so many things. Game changer.

Other People's Energy

But what about other people's energy, which I am certainly *not* the boss of, although I very much wish I was sometimes? (Kidding, kind of.)

What about friendships? Listen, we are closing in on our time together, and there are lassies who have written entire books on friendships, specifically adult female ones. Of course, we need a book on friendships. Please do read *Platonic* by Marisa Franco, PhD.

My superpower of knowing people's energy has made friendships a little challenging for me at times. I've tended to gravitate toward lassies in need. I am always happiest listening to lassies and thinking of solutions to help them.

One small snag is not everyone wants your solutions. A lot of the time, they want venting and no solutions. A rule my husband and I have that I like is I have to ask, are you asking for my advice or just need an ear? But in friendships, well, the water feels murkier. I have not figured this out, lassies; but I do have some rules around friends, which I have developed over the last few years. These have... well... changed a lot of my circles and how I show up for friends and how I know if someone is a friend or acquaintance.

One day, my friend called me, crying. She said a group of mums were just being mean, that she couldn't take it anymore. Later that day, we talked. I asked her if she wanted me to listen or give advice. She blew her nose, laughed, and said, "Go on then, coach me, Coach Mummabear."

I wish this was the only friend who either showed up at my door crying, called me crying, or left a venting voice note, because of an adult female situation. I will be honest, lassies, it's disappointing to me that I need to write this part of the book, because, frankly, I think, as a collective, we can do better. *But again*, we can't control other people's energies. We can, however, control who we are around.

I don't partake in adult female drama. I left high school a long time ago. But I have two things of importance here to say:

1: Well, the good news, the *great* news, lassie, is this: *It's not about you.* You see, the way people act, react, and behave are actually all about them and their insecurities. Ninety-nine percent of the time, it has zero to *do* with you.

2: The second thing I want you to think about is how do you feel before you see them? How do you feel during? And how do you feel after? So often, we just think about how we feel in people's company. The truth is, our body starts creating those feelings oftentimes before and after.

"Well, I feel crappy. I just feel crappy after being around them," my friend cried.

When you are sensitive, you feel other people's energies. Their reactions come before their words, and often, when they do use words, you know it's false, as you can sense their energy.

I would like to rewrite the old saying, "It's not what you say, it's how you say it." To something like this: "It's not what you say, it's the energy around you."

Highly sensitive people, which many high-performers are, notice tones of voices, body language, and facial expressions. Highly sensitive people are like the parent you can't get anything by. Granny Bel, my mum, still today knows me at thirty-nine. She knows when I'm off or bothered. As a teen, I had no chance of getting anything by her. Highly sensitive people notice bad energy and sneaky or manipulative people. This is why they UnFollow words and Follow energy.

It's really a superpower to cut to the core of who people are and what they are about. Do their words match their energy? Or did you just catch the eye-roll, followed by a deep sigh? I know I did.

Sunshine Lollipop

But then, Sunshine Lollipop entered my life, and I didn't know how much I needed it, until it was there.

What is Sunshine Lollipop, you ask? Well, her real name is Lourdes Hester. She is married to Ryan Hester and is mother to the most amazing ten-year-old, Evan Hester. She is literal sunshine.

Despite the fact our kids went to the same preschool and her home is a couple hundred yards from mine, we were never close. Niceties in Publix and at drop-off and pick-up, but I didn't know much about her.

One day, she called me and said she would love to have my boys come over to play and she'd love to have Evan play with the kids. I said I would love that, and I knew my boys would, for sure. Truth is, not many people invite three boys to their home, because—well, three boys. But she did. Literally nothing makes me appreciate a person more than when they are kind to my kids. People who focus on the kids over the adults, those are my people.

How do I feel before, after, and during my time with her? I feel like myself. I can be Melissa. Most of the time, we laugh. Sometimes, we cry. Sometimes, we take our kids to The Magical Lakehouse, and Lourdes spends seventeen hours detangling fishing rods. Sometimes, we make plans about our trip to Scotland and the joy of seeing our kids golf together. Sometimes, we create playlists, and sometimes we explain to our kids about the Britney and Justin saga and teach them the words to "Ain't No Mountain High Enough." Sometimes, Lourdes takes my kids on one-on-one dates, to show them the love. Sometimes, Evan sleeps over in the fourth bunk, and my boys fight over who sits with Evan at dinner.

It's sunshine and lollipop time. *It's Living!* And it's the greatest example to our bairns of what a friend's family can look like.

You see, if you are feeling exhausted, needing to hide from humanity, after you spend time with someone, it's time to address it. If you're anxious before or after time with someone, it's time to address.

**You see, the truth is,
the lassie or lad with the most energy wins.**

Getting to the root of where you spend your energy and why will change your life. When you start asking questions with excitement about what kind of friendships you want. What family members feed your soul. How you show up for your people. Where the energy jar is going each day. Then, everything changes.

When you start to *Follow* people's energy and *UnFollow* their words, it's easier to determine where the joy of ONE.Life is for you. What lights your soul, who lights your soul, and why? What if, on purpose and with intention, you choose wisely where your energy goes?

?

THE WORK

Follow The Energy

"I can feel you before I can hear you."
—Unknown

"Your energy introduces you before you even speak."
—Unknown

o One thing I plan to do this year to increase my physical energy is:

o I've noticed lately I have negative energy, and one way I can get back on the beam is:

o Your Mason jar is full to the brim with water. How do you plan to spend it today?

o What are some ways you can get off the beam as you transition from activity to activity?

o How do you want your energy to be when you show up today?

o How do you plan to get that energy and keep it?

o What are some solutions to get you back on the beam?

o Think about a friendship that is causing you some friction - ask yourself how do you feel before, after and during being around them?

o Are those feelings and emotions ones you desire in a friendship?

o What emotions and feelings do you desire in a friendship?

o Do you have a Sunshine Lollipop friendship?

o If you answered no, what would a Sunshine Lollipop friendship feel like, look like?

o What ways can you protect your energy when you are around people with conflicting energies?

o What relative or relationship drains your energy and why?

o How can you protect your energy in that relationship?

o Write all the ways being sensitive to other people's energies can help you win at your ONE.Life:

？

CHAPTER 19

UnFollow Decision Fatigue

"If you want to make better decisions, make fewer of them."
—James Clear

*W*hat do you want for Mother's Day, babe? I am at the store
with the kids.

The text popped up, obnoxiously staring at me, waiting for
me to respond. Texts aren't the boss of me, yet here I was,
staring, as if somehow my eyes could respond for me.

I took a deep breath and let out a sigh.

I am trained to pause when agitated.

I paused. Internally, I could feel my temperature rising. My
jaw clenching. Why was I so annoyed by that text, you wonder.
Perhaps you wonder. Or perhaps you know. Perhaps you have
had similar texts. Either way, let me explain my agitation.

I started frantically texting back, my fingers moving faster
than my brain could translate the message.

You know what I want? You know what I really
want? I want to make zero decisions for an entire day.
AN ENTIRE DAY! A whole day of not picking what or
where we eat, not deciding the time we eat. Not deciding
the activities we do or when we do them. I want a day
where the only, and I mean ONLY decisions I make are
about myself.

The little text bubble popped up, went away, popped up...
Then nothing...

My husband had chosen a wise path: zero words are likely better than whatever he began to say and then quickly decided he wanted to live one more day.

Now, you mummabear rolling her eyes and thinking how selfish I am, know that I see you and I get where you're coming from. I genuinely do. And also—this is my truth.

We make 35,000 decisions a day. It's horrifying, I know, but not really surprising, is it?

The number-one reason clients want to quit their jobs, side hustle, or company startup is not that they aren't brilliant or talented or have great ideas. No. It's burnout, and it's burnout from decision fatigue.

> **It's burnout.**
> **And it's burnout from decision fatigue.**

Think about this: you wake up in the morning, and the quality of your decisions is high. You make your green smoothie with collagen protein powder and off you go. As the day goes on, the quality of our decisions deteriorates, meaning the quality goes down.

The reason many of us eat something less than nutritional come 9 p.m. is we have made so many decisions all day, we have nothing left to give. So, we make impulse decisions, not because we suck, are weak, or have failed yet again, but because we are humans whose brains are maxed-out on decisions.

After being bothered that I felt this way about Mother's Day, I decided to research decision-making. Shocking, I know, but since research is one of my superpowers, it felt only right. I decided, if this was a big struggle in my life, it likely was in my clients' lives, too, and I was right. I started talking to my clients a lot about decisions, how they make them, and perhaps more importantly, when they make them.

The struggle of asking for help, the struggle of saying no, the inability to optimize decisions, the lack of focus and sleep, and us not habituating decisions had led us all here. Collectively agitated. Collectively maxed-out on decision-making.

Me, here I was, ticked off that I was being asked what I would like for a gift? A *gift!*

But, ticked off I was.

Side note: did you know that, today, mummabears spend more time on childcare and domestic work than mums in the 1960s, despite most of us also being in the workplace? Simple fact is this, lassies and lads, it's not just the physical energy it takes to take the bins out (the trash); it's the energy of knowing they need to be taken out. It's invisible. How do we make the invisible visible?

Now, as we move to have entrepreneurial lives and side hustles, the archaic notions that women can and are better at doing it all is not only false, it is, more importantly, leaving women struggling with the emotional labor, mental load, second shift, and invisible labor. Whatever term you use, the problem remains the same: burnout is right around the corner, waiting for us.

Burnout is the driver, but decision fatigue is the annoying backseat driver.

So often, my clients feel that, since they make less money, can get things done quicker, and are great at multitasking, then they should take it all on.

Essentially, they believe they should work like you have no kids, and, at home, act like you have no job.

My husband and my couple's therapist, Dr. Deborah Brown, tell us that we must not have these discussions when cognition is low and emotion is high. Let's be real: it's not really a discussion when those factors exist; it's an argument.

Can you just do the dishwasher?

I thought you were cooking dinner!

Doesn't land quite the same as, "Hey, when do you have time this weekend to sit down and review the week coming up and go over kids' schedules, chores, and travel?"

I wanted to help my clients with decisions—but how? I had done the research, but how could I best serve?

"I am just so frustrated. I can feel the resentments building up. I am going to explode," my client Claudia exclaimed in our session.

Claudia is a badass boss lady who has a team of fifty. Her team is the top-ranked team in the country in the company, and she has several amazing kids at home and a great husband. A recent promotion has her killing it at work.

She loves her work so much. But Claudia is struggling to keep her head above water. With aging parents and a husband whose job includes travel, plus homework, dinner, and work—it is all too much.

Claudia and I have worked together for over a year. She is a high-performer in the truest form and one of the most coachable clients I have ever worked with. She could show you her values in her calendar. She has skillfully learned the art of saying *no* and has mastered her ability to authentically ask for help. #Winning.

But here is the harsh reality of being *A Mum And...* Over fifty percent of us are divorcing and twenty-five percent of us are doing it over, "What's for dinner?"

Over twenty-five percent of us are divorcing over "What's for dinner?" Read that again.

Household chores are destroying our families, because we take the view that we will handle it all ourselves or we argue about them when emotion is high and cognition is low.

I started to see a theme in my working mum clients, and the theme was *dinner!*

Dinner! What's for dinner? Over and over, I heard this same struggle from these high-performance clients. The, "D" word wasn't divorce; it was *dinner.*

❓

Except it's not about dinner. It's never about the thing we think it is. I wanted to get to the root of the issue. It's Decision Fatigue!

It's that, by 6 p.m., our decision quality is low, and we are fatigued. Imagine being at the gym for three hours. You start off with strong reps, great quality reps; you're killing it. A few hours in, you're tired, your muscles hurt, and you can't do one more rep.

This is how our brains work with decisions.

As soon as I see patterns in my clients' reasons for falling off the beam, I tackle it by creating tools and providing practical actionable steps. But first, what is the foundational work to making good decisions? Decision-making is easier when you master asking for help, when you learn to say no, and when your sleep is a priority.

Asking for Help and Saying *No*

Okay, truth bomb. I have done actual online courses on how to say no, when to say no, who to say no to, and how to be in the No Club. I wish this was a joke. Here are the nuts and bolts of everything I've learned.

When you know your worth and believe in yourself, you can say no much easier. When you practice saying no with smaller things, it gets easier to say no with larger things. The same rules apply for asking for help.

But, as a recovering people-pleaser, I have found that most of us get so much better at this when we do the work in this book. When we begin to take our ONE.Life, chapter by chapter, and ask questions with excitement! When we dive into what we seek to *UnFollow* and redefine what to *Follow*.

Sleep

"Sleep is the best medication."

—Dalai Lama

I have read every book that has ever been written on sleep. Maybe not every one of them, but a lot. I have read all the studies, of which there are many, and below is what I learned, so you don't have to use a hundred-plus hours of your ONE.Life to read about sleep. Here is expert sleep advice from a non-expert who needed to master the art of sleep for herself, her sanity, and her clients.

If you sleep good, you feel good. Earth shattering, I know.

I have a sign in my house that I had custom-made:

> ### SLEEP GOOD,
> ### FEEL GOOD

I am a drill sergeant about sleep for my kids and myself. From a recovering insomniac, remember, not a sleep expert, here are the things you need to know.

Every morning, go outside with no sunglasses on, to kick-start your circadian rhythm. This is essentially an internal alarm clock. Do the same at night, as the sun goes down. I read nineteen research papers on that. You're welcome. For more, Follow @thehubermanlab, who is quite possibly the smartest man on the Internet.

Sleep with your devices in another room. No, seriously, do it. If @melrobbins does it, we should all do it!

Keep your room as cold as you can. Each of my kids and I have personal fans aside our bed. We aren't playing about sleep in this house.

Darkness helps with keeping your room cool and also keeps your internal alarm clock accurate.

No TV or phones one hour before bed. I've yet to master this one a hundred percent, but everything I've researched said this is a huge deal.

Every night, before I snuggle my kids to sleep, I say, "Sleep good, feel good." They hate it and usually yell back, "Sleep bad, feel good!" Parenting is such a joy, isn't it?

In all seriousness, whenever my clients are struggling, one thing I am constantly checking in on is where is your sleep at? Are you on the beam or off the beam? It is truly a miracle drug. I don't need to get into the vast number of health benefits of sleep here; the feeling benefits alone should have you thinking about sleep differently.

Do you want to feel good? Then sleep. Thank you for attending my TED Talk.

Sleep is the miracle drug that can turn feelings of "this is impossible" into "I think I got this."

Claudia had mastered sleep, too. She had sleeping mastery, along with good journaling habits, and was eating good to feel good. So, what was making her feel like she was failing? Like she couldn't handle life on life's terms?

After eighteen months of working together, so much had changed for Claudia. She felt happier than she ever had. She landed a new job of her dreams, a huge promotion. She even had a killer assistant. Her kids were healthy and happy in school. Her parents finally settled in the U.S. from Argentina and were close to her and her family. Her husband had a new job and was thriving.

Yet, *what's for dinner* was a source of pain.

The truth is, it wasn't about dinner. It wasn't about sleep or values or saying no. It was plain, old, ugly decision fatigue.

Often, this is not an area I typically start with, when working with clients, because, without value work, perfectionism work, parent-pleasing, boundary work, and the other chapters we have tackled thus far, this feels like a moot point.

*"Reducing the need to make decisions about trivial matters is
like emptying your backpack on a long hike."*
—Timothy Ferriss

The truth is the answer lies in habituating decisions.

The truth is, the answer lies in outsourcing to our subconscious.

What do I mean?

With 35,000 decisions a day, it's important to note that most of our actions, emotions, and behaviors are run by our subconscious. And by most, I mean ninety-five percent. Knowing this is power for us, as it allows us to start habituating decisions in a way we want to think, act, and do, and then to outsource them to our subconscious.

> **Habituating Decisions = Outsourcing
> Decisions to Your Subconscious.**

You still with me?

Okay, let me take my research lawyer hat off and explain this in real-life examples.

What's for dinner? Who is cooking it? At what time will it be cooked? Are we missing any ingredients? Should I oven cook? Stovetop? Microwave? Air fryer? Should we order in? What does everyone want to eat? Do they even like this meal? Or should I pick something else to cook?

Making all of those decisions at 6 p.m. is a short bus ride to the mental asylum. No, seriously. The quality of our decisions at 6 p.m., if you are up at 5 or 6 a.m., is significantly lower than, say, in the morning or, better still, the Sunday before, when one could make a meal plan for the week.

Claudia and I went through to make a plan of areas we could outsource and who would help her with these decisions and when. Several hours of planning—outsourcing—staves away pure misery at 6 p.m. for her and her family.

- Who will cook this week?

- List 5 meals for the upcoming week

- Who will grocery shop for the items and when?

- Who cleans up after dinner this week?

- What time will dinner be this week?

For Claudia and her family, these questions needed to be answered on a Sunday. If her husband was traveling, he would batch cook and freeze; then, Claudia only needed to pull the meal out of the freezer and maybe toss a salad or add some greens as a side. She wasn't, at 6 p.m., standing there, looking inside her fridge and staring at it like, somehow, the fridge would tell her the answer and the dinner would cook itself.

Once Claudia mastered this, we moved onto outsourcing other areas of her life.

There are no longer fifteen decisions on when, where, and how she will fit in workouts. Instead, they are at the same time and place each week. No more mental energy is used up here. Thus, she is no longer constantly decision-fatigued and on the verge of burnout.

In the morning, it can feel easy to pick our clothes, but if you need to run home and quickly change for a dinner event or cocktail event, the decision is much harder. Much like the fridge, how many times have you stood in front of your closet, thinking what should I wear, and feeling like everything doesn't fit.

One way I personally tackled this was buying a clothes rack. Okay, fine, I bought two, but in my defense, clothes are fun for me. Each week, I change out what is on my two clothes racks, and those are my clothes for the week. Workout gear, evening events, date night, and school drop-off gear, it's all there. Even shoes are matched under the outfits. I am not rummaging through my closet at 6 p.m. to change for the team dinner or for my kid's golf or baseball lessons. I'm ready. It's quick. Easy. No decision fatigue required.

Claudia needed to get comfortable being uncomfortable.

She needed to *UnFollow* comfortable and *Follow* uncomfortable, much like she did the day I challenged her on my retreat to do category 4 whitewater rafting, while the snow came down on us and our hands were so cold, we had to stop and build fires to heat up our hands, because we just couldn't row anymore. True story.

Hard conversations were needed with her family and herself. They were not fun. But the results sure were.

On the other side of this work, lassies and lads, is a life that is beyond your wildest dreams. It is a life that you created intentionally, on purpose.

When you become not only willing, but willing to be uncomfortable for a season, growth awaits you.

This book is all about choosing to UnFollow the comfort zone. None of this work is comfortable to us, none is second nature, and very little has been taught to us. Most of us are, for the first time, stepping down from Martyrdom Mountain, UnFollowing parent-pleasing and self-imposed prisons, and instead choosing to *Follow* a new way, a better way. A way that requires us to question everything with excitement!

Imagine ONE.Life where family dinner was your greatest joy each day. Changing for your team dinner was fun and easy. A life where workouts didn't feel like a chore but were simply on the calendar. A life where families didn't divorce over asking, "What's for dinner?"

When you question everything with excitement, the impossible feels possible.

Sometimes, that ONE.Life, requires us to have hard conversations about who does what and when in our home. Sometimes, it requires whitewater rafting. Either way, the ONE.Life you want lives on the other side of your comfort zone.

❡

THE WORK

Follow Outsourcing Decisions

o What areas of your life do you find yourself continually struggling with?

o How can you habituate these in order to outsource some decisions to your subconscious?

When we create habits like I walk every Monday at 7:00 a.m., we essentially outsource several decisions, like when you walk, what type of exercise, and who you exercise with. This process of outsourcing decisions is a preventative measure that will keep decision fatigue at bay.

o Pick one of those areas and list ways you plan to outsource them.

o Who will you discuss this with, and how will they help?

o When will you begin this new way of outsourcing?

o What excites you most about this area being outsourced?

o What uncomfortable conversation will you need to have to make this a reality?

o Why is this uncomfortable discussion worth it?

o List one way you will challenge yourself this year and do something you have never done before. P.S. Mine, this year, was to write this book. Last year was a marathon. Do something that scares your soul.

o List three ways that excite you on the other side of this work.

o Write about a time you have been uncomfortable for a season and why it was worth it?

o Write a time you stayed in your comfort zone and regretted it. What would you do differently this time?

CHAPTER 20

UnFollow Everyone

"The reason we struggle with insecurity is because we compare our behind the scenes with everyone else's highlight reel."
—Steve Furtick

'Twas the night before school started, sweet summer had ended.

Eleven whole weeks of bliss. Nine weeks of no camps where I was Team Entertainment, while running my company, writing a book, and mostly solo, due to my husband's career as a killer trial attorney. I've repeatedly told him to start losing, so people stop hiring him, but here we are.

I quickly glanced through my Insta stories and saw the darling night-before-school-starts posts (gosh, I wish you could hear my tone), and there they are.

A page I Follow had set up a special surprise table with large inflatable toys and matching table settings with each of their kid's name handcrafted into a piece of wood, and little notes. "Lord, help me," I thought out loud. "I'm just trying to shower these four and make them brush their teeth, so kids don't make fun of the plaque that's been building up over the summer."

In summer, I'm typically met with, "I brushed my teeth yesterday. Do I really need to brush every day?"

"Can I just jump in the pool instead of the shower?"

Listen, in the summer, our hygiene level shifts mostly, because I'm decision-fatigued around 3 p.m. (see previous chapter). But this was the night before school, and we would brush our teeth and wash our hair, even if I had to go in the shower with them.

My job, amongst other things in my home, is closing down the house for the night. I closed all the doors, not because I have OCD, but because my 120-pound bullmastiff likes to crap on the carpet and mark his territory while we sleep. So, I close the doors to contain the area in which he craps—true story. I locked all the doors, put the alarm on, and lowered the temp in the house to 69. Don't tell my husband—a small battle of wills occurs nightly in our home about what temperature is appropriate, paired with the not-so-small item of the AC bill.

I am typically the first one up at 5 a.m. My alarm went off, and I got up and walked into the kitchen. I instantly noticed the door to the upstairs den was open, and Munro, my "only a mother could love" dog was not in his bed. I felt my temperature start to rise, and I unclench my jaw and took a breath before heading up there to what I could only imagine was a horrific poop and pee. Happy 5 a.m. to me.

There he was, wagging his large tail side-to-side like he does and literally smiling at me, like, "Sorry, not sorry, Mum, but you used to let me sleep up here with my brothers and now you don't—but look at me now."

I smell pee, but, of course, on the cream carpet throughout the den, where three boys slept. It was impossible to spot where, and, well, it was 5 a.m. All the boys were asleep in their bunks.

I looked around and didn't see any poop. A huge sigh of relief, because, well, cleaning up said poop at 5 a.m. really is a crap way to start the day. Pun intended.

Fast forward to 8 p.m. that night. 'Twas the night before the first day of school.

Showers had been taken, teeth had been brushed, and it was time for that magical night before school starts. I tucked in blankets all around the bunk, so they had dark, cozy caves—

magical for reading our books. Their night lights were ready. They were ready.

I, like every other mother, did my last sweep of clothes and towels up off the floor, because apparently my children are animals and just leave things on the floor, and I am a moron as I continue to pick them up. I placed the items at the top of the stairs, so I could grab them on my way downstairs and do a final load of laundry before bed, like I do every night.

I went to pick up this blue, soft, fuzzy blanket of my son's. I am always washing their blankets, mostly because: 1. I love the smell of clean blankets—hello, Buff City Soap; and 2. My kids love it, too. We often smell our clean clothes and bed duvets with pure joy. It really is the small things.

My husband says my obsession with smell is crazy and I have some sort of special smelling skills. He is right: I need candles lit in my house and essential oils diffused. I'm frequently burning Palo Santo, and if I'm out by the pool, I am sure to put a load in the dryer with wool dryer balls infused with lavender, so I can smell it outside by the pool instead of my dog's poop—yes, he poops outside, too.

Throughout the day, I could smell wafts of poo and pee seeping from the den down to the stairs—but I'd checked, twice. Nothing. There was no sign of poop, and I'd cleaned up the pee. Since apparently no one else notices smells like I do, I asked the kids if they smelled poo, and everyone laughed. "You and your smells, Mum." We laughed. They were right.

My kids love blankets—we all do. No one would ever cozy up in our house without a blanket. This particular blanket was my son's favorite; it's blue with little dogs on it and super-soft. As I went to pick it up, I got a whiff of poop. The blanket wasn't lifting up. It was heavy. *Why is it heavy?* I wondered.

And there it was. All over the soft, dog-embezzled, blue blanket: *poop*. All under the blanket: *poop*. It looked like a herd of cattle had crapped on my carpet. Beside the blanket was a large trampoline. The den of the house is a "jump around, be crazy" area for my kids. It is where they wrestle and jump off furniture and do flips off trampolines. It's where they can be *boys* in my house.

I looked at the trampoline!

I looked at the blue blanket!

Back at the trampoline!

My brain was confused!

The smell!

The trampoline.

A few minutes lapsed.

OMG!

They had been jumping *off* the trampoline *onto* the blue blanket!

And now the poop was glued to our cream carpet.

The kids swarmed around me. "What is it, Mum?"

Then one kid said, "Mum, what can I get? How can I help?"

Help? Clean up poop? I thought to myself. Never in the ten years of raising this kid had he ever volunteered to pick up the poop from his dog. In fact, he is the one who gags the most, whenever we even mention the words, *dog, poop,* and *help.*

Confused again, my brain is struggling. It was after 8 p.m. now. After 8 p.m., the kids know my jar of energy is at the end, and I am much less kind or nice around this time. My conscious and playful parenting expires around this time. My kids are aware of this fact, as is my husband. This is in our family bylaws.

Wait!

Wait!

Nooooooo!

He wouldn't!

"Wait, Gray, did you cover this poop up with the blue blanket?"

His big, beautiful, brown eyes and bushy eyebrows stared back at me.

"Gray, remember the most important thing to Mumma? Trust. I can't trust you, if you aren't truthful with me."

❣

He looked at me and said these words: "Mum, it was 3 a.m., and I couldn't handle the smell of it, so I put the blanket over it. I am sorry, I forgot. Can I get something to help clean it up?"

I take a deep breath. You know the type, where you close your mouth and breathe through your nose and exhale very, very slowly. Yes, that kind. As a reminder, my amazeballs reader, remember that I am on the tail-end of nine weeks, no camps, four kids, writing this book, and being mostly solo, while traveling with these bairns around Georgia, South Carolina, North Carolina, and Tennessee. I was ready for school, even if they were not.

I love summer and the adventures of whitewater rafting, and tubing and exploring with these crazy, amazing kids of mine. But my fun meter was empty, and again, it was after 8 p.m. Did I mention all four were starting at a new school? So, new uniforms, new apps, new teachers, new drop-off times, new friends. It all started in the morning.

I thought to myself, "This is *not* how this is supposed to be."

And therein lies the problem, lassies and lads.

My stinking thinking had me believing that every home or every family of four kids is setting tables and writing notes and handcrafting names into wooden name tags with gifts waiting for their children on the first day of school. It's false advertising. But not only that, it's *not* my ONE.Life.

It won't ever be *my* life.

Why? Well, I'm the mum who buys birthday goodie bags from the Dollar Tree. I'm the mum who orders twenty pizzas for a birthday party and a Publix cake. My life's savings go to travel, and while I have rented the odd water slide for a birthday party, I tend to use our money to travel with the kids, to open their eyes to the world. At their age, I had never even left Scotland, so it makes my mumma heart happy to travel with them and my husband.

And yet, here I was, comparing myself to some Instagram page belonging to someone I don't even know. There I was, thinking, "I am doing it wrong," or "I need to do better." But here is the raw, real, honest truth.

It's time to *UnFollow* everyone and *Follow* yourself. It's time for me to join each of you on that journey. To stop the comparison. To stop seeking answers outside yourself, and instead to know what is right for us and that we are doing the best with what we have.

Gray and I cleaned up the poop. By then, it was 8:45 p.m.

My eldest was starting middle school. Tonight was a big deal.

"Mum, can you read with me?" said middle-schooler asked.

Listen, when your middle-schooler invites you into the cave inside his bed to snuggle and read, it doesn't matter if it's 8:45 p.m. anymore.

"I would love that, Cannon." We snuggled up and put his little nightlight on. That moment, right there in his little bed cave, with a nightlight and book—*that* is living. I soaked it in.

Only momentarily, of course... because....

I smelled poop again.

I reminded myself—internally, of course—to be where your feet are, Mumma.

I thought to myself, "Mummabear, it's because you just cleaned it up.'

"Cannon, do you smell poop?"

"No, Mum," he said in a very middle-schooler voice. You know the voice.

I got back to reading and snuggling.

Then, out of the corner of my eye, on the sole of Cannon's foot, *poop!* He literally had poop on his foot, in the bed.

Somehow, it had spread to Cannon's pillow and his duvet—you know, the one I'd *just* washed to smell nice for the first day of school. Yup, the same one.

The kids swarmed me, and I looked at them, saying these words, "*I'm gonna lose it!*"
They looked at me. I looked at them!
We all, in sweet synchronicity, *laughed out loud*.
It wasn't *your* night before school, but it was ours. It was perfectly imperfect, and it was us. We all hugged, and I finally got to read stories with these amazing young men of mine. And yet again, I was humbled to the reality of four kids, a large dog, and a turtle.

Once upon a time, I sought answers outside myself more than I did inside myself. Once upon a time, it was calls to my mentor, my coach, my husband, my sister, and my mum before even asking myself if I knew the answer. It's a habit many of us need to break in order to live peacefully inside our own skin. It's a habit that, when broken, creates confidence inside us around what we are capable of. It's a habit that, once deleted, we stop looking at social media and comparing our life to others.

My client recently asked me how I knew she was growing. I told her how, last week, she'd told me she had sorted something out with her boss without calling her sister, her mum, and her bestie. She knew the answer that was best for her and what to do, because she had done the work with me for over twelve months and been on several of my retreats. She'd stopped following everyone and started following herself. There is no greater sign you are on the right path than when you start asking the questions to yourself. When you have started questioning everything with excitement!

The truth is, we are a very smart generation—quite possibly the most intuitive and self-aware in the history of time. We know exactly what answer we will get from certain people, and we seek them out accordingly.

I have a coach, a therapist, a mentor, a husband, a mum, a sister, and a best friend. And I love to hear that my clients have people like this in their lives, too. The roles they play enrich my life. Their unique abilities to help me see things I cannot see have changed my life. But when we overuse these amazing people, we stop listening to ourselves. We become stuck, unable to figure things out, and we stop trusting ourselves.

When I was deciding to adopt, I knew I would be met with pushback from certain people, since I had gone through the trauma of my son having stage 4 cancer, and people would judge me for taking on something else. I remember a parent asking me why I was taking on a child with special needs, when I already had a son who'd battled cancer. Perhaps there was no mean spirit in his words, but once upon a time, this people-pleasing perfectionist may have taken that word and changed her mind.

But as I write this chapter, I see that our little decision to adopt, our Charlie Mary Emma Wiggins, *jumps* into the pool as her three brothers cheer her on. I knew. My husband knew!

As smart a generation as we are, we are also a generation who has lost our ability to Follow ourselves.

Our insides and outsides don't match, because we have lost trust in ourselves.

We have lost it by following everyone over ourselves. Instead, many of us have chosen to live our lives for others and not ourselves.

Are you living your life for you and your family, or for others?

If you don't trust yourself, you don't love yourself. Building the muscle of trust allows following yourself to become the new way, a new habit.

Choosing to UnFollow everyone and then *Follow You* is an act of saying I respect your opinion, but I trust myself! And if I am wrong, it is just one more opportunity to learn.

The time is now to question everything with excitement and know that the ONE.Life you seek begins with the simple choice to UnFollow everyone and start to Follow you.

❦

❣

THE WORK
Follow You

---

*"Trust yourself. Create the kind of self that
you will be happy to live with all your life."*
—Golda Meir

o Where in your life do you see yourself often comparing
   your life with others? Vacations, mothering, marriage,
   work? How do you feel when you do this?

o What area of your life do you need to seriously lower
   expectations of yourself?

o What area do you often look to others for advice? Do
   you take their advice over your own often? Why? How
   does it feel when you do that?

o What if you started asking yourself the answer to the
   questions *before* you discussed it with others? How
   would this make you feel?

o Who do you always call when you don't know the
   answer? Why do you call them?

o   How does it feel to pause and think through your answer, your solution, before adding noise to the problem?

o   What benefits would you gain in your life by choosing to UnFollow everyone and instead decide to Follow YOU?

o   If you continue to not develop the muscle of self-trust, where will your life be in five years?

o   If you develop the muscle of following *you,* where will you be in five years?

o   What thing have you wanted to do but are scared of what people will say? Which person in particular?

o   What if you did the thing, knowing you were following yourself, and even though it would be hard at first, it was the first step to building trust in you? How would this feel?

ACKNOWLEDGMENTS

YOU DID IT!!! You read the book. YOU did THE WORK. You deserve what is coming next for you. It takes time and commitment and no doubt things are already changing in your ONE.Life. I would like to take a moment and thank the people in my life that made it possible for you to have the transformational journey you just had. Without them this would not have been possible and they are the true ones who deserve the accolades.

Writing a book while raising bairns, and also running several companies of my own with a husband who travels, is not for the faint of heart. Don't you dare let any of those much-more-established-than-me authors convince you otherwise—they are all liars. My clan, the Wiggins Clan, sacrificed every Saturday with me, as I went on sixteen-mile training sessions. They have stood at the finish line of a 26.2-mile marathon with massive signs saying, "Love you, Mum!" And they sacrifice full days while I write my weekly quota of words.

The lessons—holy permission slip, lassies and lads—imagine the permission I am giving those bairns! Permission to have a family and live your ONE.Life: bravery-building much! I am A Mum And...

You can be A Mum And... is tattooed on my soul. Even though I am tattoo-less, I am sure this is what my life's mission is. It takes a special family to support the type of mum and wife they have. Thank you, Wiggins Clan! No one loves you more than me. I would *Outlander*-style go to war for you! Jaime and Claire have got nothing on our love story.

At this point, you may have gathered I'm Scottish and an *Outlander* fan, but you should also know I'm a fan of lassies and lads winning at life. I live and breathe that daily, and my family are the reason I am able to. My life's mission lives inside and outside the Wiggins Clan. Thank you to sexy legs (at least that's how he is listed on my phone). He is also my husband, baby daddy, and teammate for some two decades. Thank you for knowing what you were getting into by marrying me and loving me anyway. Thank you for giving up easy Sundays for me—I cannot imagine anything more romantic. My ability to serve is because of the Wiggins Clan, and I am hopeful you meet some of these freaking superstars at every signing table at every event I keynote. You will fall madly in love with them and probably like them more than me!

Cannon, my muse for living: I have yet to meet a braver young man than you. You made me a Mumma, and I have never been the same since. ONE.life: What're you going to do it with it?—is all because of you.

Arran, you're as good looking on the outside as you are on the inside. You and I are the same person—I am sorry buddy, but it's true. You are me, and I am you. Our mutual understanding of each other makes our bond unbreakable. Smart and handsome... Watch out, world! If you are not on some stage or TV screen somewhere someday, I will be shocked. You have never met a stranger, and it feels like my gran's genes run right through your heart of gold.

Gray, you care so deeply about all of us. You are an anchor in our family! Sports are your life, and you and your dad's bond over sports is one of the greatest joys of my life. Thank you for allowing me to be the mum who yells too loud and embarrasses you at every game. You are a sports superstar, and you can be whatever you want, buddy. Never forget that. I love you so much.

Charlie, my princess. I love that we laugh at all the same jokes. I love that we are birthday twins. I love that you ask me for hugs every day and just randomly tell me I am the best mum and you love me. Your heart is massive, as is your brain. You're amazing. You are a born leader, and watching you grow is one of my favorite life activities.

Olivia, my stepdaughter, whom I met when you were seven. How are you twenty-five with a baby? I cannot even. Time went too fast. But I treasure every volleyball game, our trip to D.C., and every time you beat me at go-carting. You made my twenties so much more fun than they would have been. Thank you for loving and accepting me, even when I wasn't always great.

To my sister, my best friend in the whole world. I've never met a better human in my life. No one compares, and thank God I only have one sister, as I couldn't handle fighting another sister to be your bestie.

To my Mum, the only example I ever needed. No one is a better mum than you. No one. You are exceptional in every way. You have had more pain than anyone I know, and yet you smile. I hope I can be even half the mum you have been to me. My Amazeballs Clients:

I want not only to acknowledge my clients, but to praise them. They are the bravest group of humans I have ever met. The fact they let me into their lives and courageously raised their hands and said yes to telling their story to help others— I can't even. It's difficult to put into words the respect and gratitude I feel for each of them. You challenge me, you make me work to be better for you, and you inspire me each and every day. This book is only possible because of you trusting me. I am deeply honored to be your coach and friend.

Lynne Mixson: I want to acknowledge Lynne Mixson, my walking buddy, who diligently and beautifully with a fine-tooth comb read every word of my first draft, correcting every grammar error, and who made sure my dyslexic spelling was corrected. This angel did it just because. Just because that is how she is. I admire her so very much for the friend she is and the woman she is.

My amazeballs friends:

Samantha Joy: I am attempting to write this through tears, as without you this book would not exist. *You* believed in me at a time in my life I was struggling to believe in me. You were the first soul to place me on the main stage as a keynote speaker, as a coach. I will never forget that. Your belief is a gift, and I love you, friend.

Amberly Lago: You catapulted me into this work by asking me to speak to your UNSTOPPABLE Mastermind. Your feedback, your push, was what I needed, and I am forever grateful. Thank *you*. I love you, friend.

Brooke Hemingway: I found myself at ALIGN, your women's conference. You asked me to do a workshop. I had never done one before, and you believed I could. You wanted more for me and my work and my message. ALIGN THE GOOD LIFE, your community, showed me I could truly be A Mum And... You continue to be a driving force in my life, and I am so grateful. I love you friend.

Lourdes Hester: for your real talk. Your, "You won't like what I am about to say" chats are life. They keep me trudging the road to a happy destiny. You are sunshine, and I am forever grateful you allow me to be your friend. I love you, friend.

To My Sober Community:

As I approach fifteen years sober – I know this book would not be here without each of you showing up and ALSO sitting your arses on the white plastic chairs, the same ones that have saved my life and made this ONE.Life possible.

Love,

Coach Mummabear
An extremely grateful Scottish lassie

KEYNOTE SPEAKING & COACHING

If you are inspired by this book and the teachings inside it, consider hiring Melissa as your next keynote speaker. You can visit her website and message her directly here:

www.melissawiggins.life

See Testimonials page for why you would consider hiring her especially if you are looking for a dynamic speaker to make your crowd laugh and cry and most importantly to have them think and act.

If Scottish accents are your thing, check out her top-ten-percent globally ranked podcast, *Coaching and a Cup of Tea with Mummabear.*

Retreats

On a more intimate level, she hosts retreats twice a year at her own home, which she calls The Magical Lakehouse, a lake house nestled in the woods at the foothills of the Blueridge Mountains: @themagicallakehouse on Instagram.

Coaching and a Cup of Tea with Mummabear

Subscribe to Melissa's top-ten-percent globally ranked podcast for your weekly dose of life changing insights and inspiration. From guest interviews to original tools this is the one to Follow!

Social Media

You can keep up with Melissa on social media:

o   On IG at @coachmummabear_

o   On Facebook under Melissa Wiggins

There, you can see her day-to-day, raising four kids, the messy middle, keynote speaking, coaching, raising money for kids' cancer, and most likely, her workout at 5 a.m. *Enjoy!*

Show Us Your Action

Melissa loves to see your work—your answers to exciting questions. Share on social using #UnFollow, but also email them to melissa@melissawiggins.life

Don't Just Read. Act

Your next empowering chapter starts with ONE.Life. Are you in?

Ready for a seismic shift in your life? *UnFollow* is just the beginning—the unbecoming, the undoing, the unfollowing of all that has constrained you. It's time to create your favorite version of your ONE.Life!

Elevate your journey by joining Melissa's ONE.Life monthly coaching subscription, featuring group and one-on-one sessions, as well as an exclusive online program packed with transformational videos.

Sign up today at melissawiggins.life/onelife.

MelissaWiggins.life

TESTIMONIALS

Keynote Speaker Testimonials

"Melissa has been our keynote speaker at the Buster Posey Twenty-eighth Annual Gala at the Oracle Stadium in San Francisco several times, each time ending in a standing ovation. The players and guests always compliment us on having her speak. How one gets you to laugh and cry in the same speech baffles us—yet she does it. If you need someone to inspire a crowd with Scottish sass and knowledge, we highly recommend Melissa."

—Buster and Kristen Posey,
San Francisco Giants MLB Player

"Melissa Wiggins has a fantastic story to share. Her message will inspire and motivate you in facing the many daily challenges that you must deal with. Yes, Melissa Wiggins is *Awesome,* baby, with a capital A!"

—Dick Vitale, ESPN Hall of Fame basketball analyst

"As a multiple cancer survivor, I always listen intently to those voices whose lives have also been deeply impacted by cancer. Melissa Wiggins is a compelling voice of authenticity as she shares her story and the emotional roller coaster of daily life, raising a family and taking care of a loved one with special needs. Each one of her presentations is designed to meet the needs of every audience, as she makes attendees think, laugh, and cry."

—Harry Rhoads, co-founder
Washington Speakers Bureau

"Melissa is the rare speaker who has the ability to move an audience and change their mindset. Passionate, funny, and engaging, this Scottish powerhouse is the perfect choice for any conference or meeting planner."
—Brant Menswar, "Top 10" Motivational Speaker, Best-selling author, *Black Sheep*

"I have had the honor and pleasure of watching Melissa Wiggins speak on many occasions and am always amazed at how she captivates her audience. This smart and funny Scottish lass will make you laugh and cry but will always inspire and motivate. I cannot recommend her highly enough as a keynote speaker. You will not be disappointed!"
—Kay Rawlins, founder & SVP, Community Relations President, Orlando City Foundation

"Melissa Wiggins is... Energy all day, every day. Influencer, fashionista, mentor, foodie, advice-giver and taker. She is one big ball of human emotions who I just want to be around! In a packed venue or in the hallway at the supermarket, when she talks, people stop and listen. Melissa is unapologetically loud, and *that* is what makes her an incredible speaker. Not only does her tone demand attention but respect, as well. Why? The lawyer babe from Scotland who has made the U.S.A. her home will not take no for an answer, on anything! This chick barely stands at five-feet tall (need to confirm), barely weighs a hundred pounds (wet!), has pushed multiple babies out her vajayjay, has enough room in her heart to adopt, has enough empathy/patience and vision to be the founder of Cannonball Kids' cancer, after the C-word came knocking, *uninvited*, and is the most verbally engaging woman I know.

"There is something about when someone looks you in the eye and there's a connection... She cares, and she wants *you* to know it. She knows her audience... moms, fashion, philanthropy, survivors, substance-abuse warriors, foodies, athletes... She speaks their language, and that's why there is such power in the spoken word from Melissa Wiggins... She's lived it, she gets it... She is us. She is you."

—Ybeth Bruzual, Spectrum News 13 anchor

"You cannot interact with and know Melissa Wiggins and not be inspired by her. She took the most heartbreaking and scary situation, the fight for her son's life, and turned it into an incredible charitable foundation that has a huge team of volunteers that help to make it happen every year. Melissa isn't afraid to be vulnerable and honest and I think that is what makes her incredibly relatable. As a life coach, Melissa brings a lifetime of experiences and lessons to the table, and she is incredibly generous with her time and willingness to share what she has learned along the way, to help others.

"I started a charitable foundation a little over a year ago, and Melissa and her team have always been willing to meet with me, answer questions, and share their best advice. Melissa is a true girl's girl, and I am so incredibly thankful to have her in my life."

—Jennifer Knopf, President, Founding Director,
Reed Charitable Foundation

Coaching Testimonials

"My sessions with Melissa have truly helped me move forward in life with a more positive spin as a 'mum,' wife, friend, and in business. She has helped me identify my values, rethink the importance of perfectionism, and is an exceptional listener. Through her witty Scottishness, Melissa digs deep, challenges, and offers wisdom to help make life less heavy.

"Melissa wants to create ripples! She really wants to create a community of people who are empowering one another. So, it meant taking what I had learned from her being my one-on-one coach to the next level, which was EMPOWERED.Life. You almost have accountability partners within your journey, and it gives you the opportunity to learn from one another. You get the accountability to push through and get in touch with yourself and dig deep.

"Since I started coaching, I've had the confidence to step off the hamster wheel for a bit, which is not like me."

—Heidi Foster, Corporate Leader

"Since I began working with Melissa, both my professional and personal lives have changed for the better! I am an entrepreneur and often get overwhelmed, but Melissa has taught me how to ensure I complete the task at hand and move forward with ease. Obtaining emotional control internally allows me to drive forward and inspire my team. The pulls of entrepreneurial life are not easy, when you have goals like I do. They required getting curious about how I made decisions and developing discipline to stay focused at the most important task.

"Using essentialism concepts with Melissa has truly helped. I have more work to do, but having Melissa to grow with me this year as I build my empire has truly made it all feel manageable. Melissa has been such a positive addition to my life, and I am so looking forward to seeing where we can go together in the future—it's exciting!"

—Olivia Myers, Founder, Overchill the Label

"One of my biggest wins is finding who I am. I got to forty thinking, *Who am I?* I couldn't even answer questions like, what is your favorite movie? What's your favorite food? I worked hard to find out what my values are, and then I had a moment of clarity and realized, 'Oh, that's me, and I am confident in it.' I now have a sense of self-compassion and confidence. I will be going back to the tools, digging deeper, and continuing to empower myself."

—Hope Theisen, Corporate Leader

"One of the greatest things about being a part of this group is being surrounded by people who are so interested in their growth and in learning more. Obviously, to be around so many people with those same intentions and desires for themselves is such a motivator for me."

—Karen Moreno, Owner, The Bar Method Winter Park

"Melissa has the ability to pull out the vulnerability in you that you might have been hiding behind."

—Jessica, Impact Social Media

"Coaching has impacted me as a dad. I am more patient, more understanding. I listen before I jump, and I'm able to connect on a different level with (my children). Melissa has the ability to sit and talk with you, give you perspectives that don't hit you at first, then you're like, wow, that's what she meant."

—Dan Gunn, Entrepreneur

"EMPOWERED.Life helped me: Focus on Growth. As a group, we are all focused in the same way, running companies or being entrepreneurs or just focusing on growth and how to be the best version of ourselves. And when you surround yourself with that type of community and those types of people, the conversations are so impactful. They're so connecting!

"Intentionality: I feel like, through coaching, my time is intentional, with every hour of my day, and that started in month one, when we started talking about our values. I wish my abdominal muscles got the exercise my brain has been getting over the last six months of coaching with Melissa.

"Thought Work: Thought reset is something that Melissa has taught us, and as a result, I am now able to say, 'No, Diana! That's not true. That thought you are thinking is not true.' Being able to have the tool to do that myself now, where before I'd let it spin in my head, is empowering for me, my family, my work, and everybody around me."

—Diana Gleason, Owner, DG Consulting Services

"EMPOWERED.Life, for me, is all about learning that I can take a pause from different things, to be able to fill myself up. And I'm not going to say 'refill,' because I don't think that I've ever been as full as I am right now! I also know that there's much more to come.

"Power of the Group: I am forever grateful that I jumped into group coaching, because my life is richer and different thanks to the relationships I have formed.

"I Love Myself: I know today, I love myself just as much as I love other people. And I think that was probably the biggest win for me, because the ripple effect is that the people around me now know that I love myself just as much as I love them. If not more.

"The Ripple Effect: When we teach other people what we've been taught, then they feel excited about it, and then they know that they can go out and do the same thing."

—Stephanie Bowman
Founder, One Heart for Women and Children

"To keep it simple, the ownership I've taken, the solutions I've created, the confidence I've grown, the empowerment I feel—all things I've gained from working with Melissa. All things we, together, have worked on. Having someone believe in me so much and support my inner and outward growth is invaluable. She is amazeballs."

Morgan Kalberger, Founder, K & Co. Interiors

ABOUT THE AUTHOR

M elissa Wiggins, a Scotland native, currently resides in Orlando, Florida. She is a proud mum of five and an advocate for change in pediatric cancer. She holds a law degree from the prestigious schools of University of Glasgow and the University of Edinburgh, and prior to moving to Orlando in 2010, she worked as a commercial litigation solicitor in her nation's capital, where she gained court experience and a background in advocacy.

When her firstborn son, Cannon James Roland Wiggins, was diagnosed with stage 4 cancer, and she was about to give birth to twins, her full-time calling for three and a half years became saving her son's life. Melissa and her husband, Michael, founded Cannonball Kids' cancer, a nonprofit pediatric cancer research foundation, in 2015. Cannon, his cancer journey, survivorship, and her family's experience inspired her to write her first book, *Thankful For the Fight,'* in which she shares her family's heartbreaking and inspiring cancer battle.

In addition to advocate, lawyer, boss, and wife, Melissa proudly wears the hats of stepmum, bio mum, adoptive mum, and, most recently, grandmother—all by age thirty-six.

Melissa is now a lawyer-turned-Master Certified Professional Coach and has since worked with countless women, men, couples, and families, encouraging and empowering them to become the favorite version of themselves—or, as she likes to say, helping them "get ripped on the inside, so that their insides match their outside."

It is said that life's hardest moments make us stronger. That is true for Melissa. As a result of advocating, fundraising, and changing the world of pediatric cancer, Melissa has had the privilege of speaking on stages across the globe, from keynoting at Glasgow Children's Hospital to the San Francisco Giants' stadium and in the private home of Dick Vitale, ESPN megastar.

Mummabear is her moniker, and it is also a metaphor. Life can be hard, but we can do hard things. Strength does not come from life being easy. Radical changes in the way we live our lives or practice medicine do not come from our silence. It comes from finding our *ROAR*. Melissa knows that, to live your truth, you must first find your voice. Her *ROAR* saved her son, changed her marriage, and transformed her ONE.Life.

Finding Mummabear came as a result of years of choosing to UnFollow. Years of looking at her life and deciding, choosing, what she would *UnFollow* and *Follow*. What societal norms, familial tendencies, and unspoken expectations she would *UnFollow* and how.

How? By questioning everything with excitement! By taking every hardship, everything she knew, and putting it through this filter of her future self. By knowing that questioning everything with excitement would be an investment toward her future—her favorite version of herself.